Praise for
Competing for Customers

"Great messages! Deliver results, or someone else will. The authors offer lots of smart concepts and practical tools that could make a real difference, especially for established players."

—**Dr. Jim Noble**, CEO of The Advisory Council
and former global CIO of Altria Group

"It's time to stop talking about 'focusing on the customer' and start doing it. B2B customers engage differently with companies today. Jeb, Amir, and Craig provide a practical blueprint for connecting with customers in the modern era."

—**Rishi Dave**, Chief Marketing Officer, Dun & Bradstreet

"A *must-read* for forward-thinking marketers who need to focus at creating customer success—and long-term, deep engagements—several steps down their value chain. The authors guide necessary and fundamental shifts in thinking for the discipline. Packed with real cases and practical How To's as well. Don't miss this one!"

—**Ralph A. Oliva**, Director, Institute for the Study of Business Markets,
Professor of Marketing, Smeal College of Business, Penn State

"The authors make it clear that delivering customer success is not an option—rather, it's a competitive necessity."

—**Vijay Govindarajan**, Coxe Distinguished Professor at
Dartmouth's Tuck School of Business

"Read this book to learn how your company can 'earn the right' to customer growth in the ever-important Subscription Economy."

—**Jeanne Bliss**, author of *Chief Customer Officer 2.0*
and President of CustomerBliss

Competing for Customers

Competing for Customers

Why Delivering Business Outcomes Is Critical in the Customer First Revolution

Jeb Dasteel
Amir Hartman
Craig LeGrande

Publisher: Paul Boger
Editor-in-Chief: Amy Neidlinger
Executive Editor: Jeanne Glasser Levine
Development Editor: Natasha Wolmers
Cover Designer: Alan Clements
Managing Editor: Kristy Hart
Project Editor: Elaine Wiley
Copy Editor: Cheri Clark
Proofreader: Laura Hernandez
Indexer: Tim Wright
Senior Compositor: Gloria Schurick
Manufacturing Buyer: Dan Uhrig

© 2016 by Jeb Dasteel, Amir Hartman, and Craig LeGrande
Published by Pearson
Upper Saddle River, New Jersey 07458

For information about buying this title in bulk quantities, or for special sales opportunities (which may include electronic versions; custom cover designs; and content particular to your business, training goals, marketing focus, or branding interests), please contact our corporate sales department at corpsales@pearsoned.com or (800) 382-3419.

For government sales inquiries, please contact governmentsales@pearsoned.com.

For questions about sales outside the U.S., please contact intlcs@pearsoned.com.

Company and product names mentioned herein are the trademarks or registered trademarks of their respective owners.

Printed in the United States of America

2   16

ISBN-10: 0-13-417220-5
ISBN-13: 978-0-13-417220-0

Pearson Education LTD.
Pearson Education Australia PTY, Limited
Pearson Education Singapore, Pte. Ltd.
Pearson Education Asia, Ltd.
Pearson Education Canada, Ltd.
Pearson Educación de Mexico, S.A. de C.V.
Pearson Education—Japan
Pearson Education Malaysia, Pte. Ltd.

Library of Congress Control Number: 2015956195

Contents

Acknowledgments

Over the past three decades, we have had the privilege of working with and advising many of the smartest and most successful global business leaders. Their vision, insights, and innovative thinking have inspired us to write this book and build a compelling platform for customer success delivery.

We especially want to thank the Oracle team, including Tony Banham, Jeremy Whyte, Lee Francescone, Carol Sato, Tim Falvey, Vandana Heda, Sheri Woolbert, and Kara Cummings; the Business Transformation Team at Cisco and particularly their leader, Sandy Hogan; GE's Ganesh Bell and Allison Lily; Rockwell's visionary CTO Sujeet Chand; Dave Coggens and Mary Brigden from Telogis; and Oracle CIO Advisory Board members Norm Fjeldheim with Qualcomm, Bill Eline with Parker Hannifin, Brian Simmermon with Subaru America, and Dave Rudzinsky with Hologic. These leaders were key contributors to helping shape and prove many of the themes in this book and were kind enough to share their experiences through the case studies we present here. Given the newness of the concepts that we've tackled, it was their confidence and perseverance that have allowed us to share their unique stories, bringing the concepts to life. We want to particularly acknowledge Mark Hurd, CEO of Oracle, for honoring us with writing the Foreword to this book, and for allowing us to share his company's story on the road to customer success.

We owe a big thanks to Jeanne Levine, Elaine Wiley, and the editorial team at Pearson/FT Press. Their guidance and patience are much appreciated. Also contributing to the concepts in the book are our colleagues at Mainstay. We would also like to pay special thanks to Rob Bracken for helping craft the narrative of the book and for delivering our ideas in a format that truly presents the essence of the message in the most compelling way. We would also like to express our gratitude to Amanda Dasteel for the amazing job with the graphics in this book. Amanda took our ideas and unintelligible scribbles and created terrific images that complement and improve on our writing.

Finally, we'd like to thank our families and friends for enduring the weekends, early mornings, and late evenings spent working on the book for the past year-plus. Their patience and support have allowed us to dedicate ourselves to completing our mission.

About the Authors

Jeb Dasteel holds the position of Senior Vice President and Chief Customer Officer at Oracle. He is responsible for driving the relentless focus on customer success into all aspects of the Oracle business. Dasteel works across Oracle to deliver customer programs that continuously improve collaboration and attainment of customer business outcomes, value delivered, and loyalty. He has been with Oracle for 17 years in a number of corporate and field-based roles. Before joining Oracle in 1998, he worked as a management consultant at Gemini Consulting, helping Fortune 500 organizations define and implement business and IT strategies.

Amir Hartman, Founder and Managing Director of Mainstay, is a leading authority on corporate and technology transformations, and works with customers to help develop and execute customer success strategies. He is an international best-selling author and has served on the Business School faculty at Berkeley, Columbia, Harvard Business School Interactive. A frequent speaker, he is the author of several influential books, most recently *Ruthless Execution* (2014). Prior to forming Mainstay, Amir served as Managing Director for Cisco System's Corporate Internet Strategy and the Internet Business Solutions Group. In this role, he was responsible for shaping Cisco's Internet business strategy and advising key customers on the same.

Craig LeGrande recently coauthored *Ruthless Execution* (2014) and serves as a senior advisor to leading high-tech companies. As Founder and Managing Director of Mainstay, LeGrande leads a world-class team helping clients deliver customer success strategies, including innovative marketing and sales enablement capabilities. Before forming Mainstay, LeGrande worked in Cisco's Internet Business Solutions Group and Accenture's Strategic Services and

Technology Services Groups. He received an MBA from the Tuck School of Business at Dartmouth College and a BS in Electrical Engineering with Honors from the University of Florida—*Go Gators*!

Foreword

We live in a world where cellphones outnumber the planet's seven billon people. Where social networkers spend 200 billion minutes networking every month. And where the Internet now surpasses TV as the media of choice. Today, consumers can make or break our products by sharing their opinions with millions in moments.

Technology is erasing all boundaries and enhancing the human experience with new services at every turn. People are rushing to immerse themselves in the possibilities, while enterprises are challenged to keep up. It's a massive market shift that is rewriting our lives, and redefining how our businesses succeed—or fail.

Like it or not, technology now plays a pivotal role in our lives. More people than ever are demanding more access to more information and services, wherever, however, and whenever they need them.

The enterprises that thrive in this world will follow that lead and look beyond the technology they have to the possibilities that technology can enable. *Competing for Customers* expertly explores the opportunities and challenges ahead for business leaders.

What will it take to succeed in this brave new world? Every business leader I talk to offers a slightly different answer. But in my experience, you can boil it down to three critical capabilities: business agility (the ability to react to new opportunities), resiliency (the ability to "survive and thrive" in tough times), and long-term financial growth (which no business leader can possibly afford to ignore).

By no means are these easy things to achieve. Just consider: Half of the companies on the Fortune 500 list in the year 2000 are no longer on the list. If we look back to 1990, 70% of that elite group fails to make the list today.

Such volatility underscores the perils of not keeping up with change. This is true not only in my industry—information technology—but in every sector that depends on technology to any significant degree. Which is to say, virtually every modern enterprise.

In the past decade I have seen massive changes shake the technology industry, starting with our customers. In short, they want more and they want it now. Our customers have come to expect great experiences in their consumer lives, where there's an app for just about everything and it works on any device. Why not expect a similarly great experience at work?

What's more, they're happy to pay for it. Research shows that 86% of consumers would pay more for a better experience. Amazingly, though, only 1% of consumers feel they actually have had a good experience.[1]

The workforce is evolving as well. Notably, our employees are getting younger: Experts say that by 2020 half of the U.S. workforce will be "millennials"—workers in their 20s and 30s. The challenge is in persuading these young and restless workers to build new skills and a promising career with your company over several years. Some 60% of this highly productive cohort may leave for new jobs in less than three years.[2]

On top of all this—and significantly for information technology—the market for business computing is shifting dramatically. Customers in this space are getting restless: 76% of executives in a recent survey say their current enterprise-resource-planning (ERP) systems—the software that runs the bulk of their business operations—are "unacceptable."[3]

For more and more of these companies, the future lies in cloud computing. In a new survey, close to half of CFOs said they plan to move their financial management systems to the cloud.[4] This mass migration of enterprise systems could be the number one trend in business today, one that *Competing for Customers* examines in detail. And as the authors rightly point out, this transition is best viewed as part of a much larger trend: the transformation of how businesses—that is, your customers—buy and consume products and services.

Thanks to the cloud, businesses increasingly prefer to rent, or subscribe to, services rather than owning operational systems outright. By doing so, companies can jettison a lot of the cost and complexity of running elaborate systems in-house and thereby become more flexible, scalable, and results-oriented than ever before.

Business leaders I talk to say the move to a service-centric world is more about focusing on competitive differentiation and business results and less about owning and operating the infrastructure needed to deliver them.

Today, when companies are buying a service, they're buying an outcome. *Competing for Customers* delves deeply into results-based buying and offers smart advice for companies seeking to measure and ensure business outcomes for customers.

In the past several years I have had the pleasure to work closely with co-author Jeb Dasteel. As Oracle's chief customer officer, Jeb helps me guide Oracle's transformation into a truly customer-centric organization, a journey detailed in this book. We understand that this is a journey with no single destination—we'll never stop listening to our customers and never stop discovering better ways to ensure their success.

Read *Competing for Customers* to find out what it takes to make customer success part of your organization's DNA. Use it as your road map for navigating the competitive landscape in what the authors call the "Customer First Revolution."

—Mark Hurd, Oracle CEO

Endnotes

[1] RightNow Customer Experience Impact Report (2012), based on a survey conducted by Harris Interactive.

[2] SHRM, 2013; Tammy Erikson, 2009; Forbes, 2013.

[3] Oracle customer survey, 2014.

[4] Oracle customer survey, 2015.

Introduction

"There is only one boss. The customer. And he can fire every-body in the company from the chairman on down, simply by spending his money somewhere else."

–Sam Walton

Is there anything really new that can be said about the customer? No doubt you've heard all the old adages before: how the customer is in charge and calls the shots; how your business is all about satisfying the customer; and how you need to stay "laser focused" on the customer.

Over the years, a lot of people have explored what makes customers tick and how paying attention to your customer fuels business success. More recently, the "customer experience" meme has been grabbing the attention of business leaders, marketers, and sales executives alike. The idea that "journey mapping" the customer's experience or identifying "moments of truth" can improve loyalty and promote customer retention is everywhere these days. But is that really sufficient?

Most companies know intuitively that pleasing customers is good for business. Businesses that sell to consumers—B2C companies like Walmart and Apple—have known this for a long time. By contrast, businesses that mainly sell to other businesses—B2Bs—have generally been slower to grasp this concept. Ostensibly, they're all for pleasing customers, but they lack either the know-how or the inclination to change tried-and-true business models, preferring to tell customers something along the lines of "this is what we're selling—take it or leave it." For these businesses, it has been mostly about closing the deal and moving to the next opportunity. Seldom do they try to find out whether the customer actually used what they had bought, whether it met expectations, or whether it actually contributed to a desired business outcome.

Lately, though, B2Bs are changing their tune. More of these organizations are paying closer attention to customer satisfaction, loyalty, and customer experience, and many have made impressive strides in measuring and analyzing crucial points in the customer "lifecycle." They want to know what their customers think and feel about their products, and what the customer's day-to-day experience is like. Many are investing heavily in systems to capture these insights.

So why do we need a new book about competing for customers?

The answer, we believe, comes down to this: Whether you know it or not, everything about how you sell to customers is changing; everything about how you market to them must be rethought; and everything about how you keep customers coming back needs a fresh look. Even the *individual* who's likely to buy your product is different.

These changes are being driven by titanic shifts in the nature of the B2B economy and in the customer relationships that underpin it. Business buyers are behaving more like consumers: better educated from the flood of information available on the Web; empowered by the ruthlessly candid sharing of opinions on social media; and emboldened by the ease with which you can switch to the competition in what is called the Subscription Economy (more about that later).

If you don't get onboard with the fundamental shifts we describe in *Competing for Customers,* you will likely face disruptions that could threaten the very core of your business.

We wrote this book to help companies take advantage of the Subscription Economy and avoid being marginalized. We wrote it to help you understand and prepare for the coming changes, and to learn from innovators who have rejuvenated their businesses by transforming how they interact with their customers. In these pages, we hope to provide you with the insights and tools you need to outcompete your rivals for customers and lay the groundwork for sustained growth and profitability.

The Subscription Economy

Revolutions in business never stop. New ones, as if sailing in on a tsunami, wash over the economy every few years. We're in the middle of one right now, and it represents nothing short of the birth of a new way of doing business. It's the Subscription Economy—and by this we mean an economy in which more and more products are designed to be consumed "as needed" or as a service and, moreover, sold not for their particular features and functions, but for the business outcomes they'll deliver.

It's no coincidence we're seeing this first in the technology industry where "software as a service" has made deep inroads into businesses ranging from mom-and-pop storefronts to Fortune 500 giants. Today it's not uncommon for companies to rent most of their software "in the cloud" to run everything from marketing, sales and HR to manufacturing and document processing. "Software," as Marc Andreesen famously said, "is eating the world."

Even old-line industries are leaning toward the subscription model. Construction equipment maker Caterpillar, for example, has started selling what one might call "mining as a service." If you're a customer, that means you rent earth-moving machines and everything you need to keep them running over a set period of time. You're no longer just buying bulldozers; you're subscribing to "bulldozer services" (or "bulldozer capacity") that allow you to manage fleet performance remotely, and help monitor and manage your operations across key areas such as equipment management, productivity, and safety.

The rise of the "as-needed economy" will have a profound—and, yes, disruptive—impact on companies of all sizes. For more and more companies, it means the selling process will be turned upside down. Rather than paying for products up front in a single capital outlay, customers will spread the purchase over years—and constantly evaluate whether the subscription is worth renewing. Under this scenario, your "sale" is no longer a one-time event but one of many interactions in which you engage in your customer's business. This is a new kind of partnership that demands hyper vigilance if you hope to retain your customers long-term.

What all this implies is a dramatic swing in the balance of power between buyer and seller. No longer saddled with big up-front capital outlays—and the business risk they pose—the customer suddenly gains more leverage and control. In the Subscription Economy, a big portion of the risk of not realizing full value from an investment shifts from the buyer to the seller, who must now think about the customer in a whole new way.

There's another dimension to what we call the Customer First Revolution. This is related to the interconnectivity of billions of individual devices known as the Internet of Things. The IoT—in which equipment and machines of all types interact with other machines (and people) in the cloud—holds tremendous potential for transforming customer relationships.

Imagine knowing whether your customers are actually using your products, how often, and in what areas of their business. Furthermore, what if you knew whether they were getting maximum value out of them? In the Subscription Economy, operationalizing these kinds of insights holds the potential to drive business value and radically transform customer relationships. Indeed, research firm Gartner has predicted that the Internet of Things market opportunity could be worth $1.9 trillion by 2020, a prediction that is looking to be right on track.[1]

How to Compete for Customers: Our Central Thesis

What we're suggesting is this: In the future, companies will no longer be able to sell, market, and service the old way. Not that you need to throw out all of those trusty truisms. "Focusing on the customer" makes as much sense today as it did in Henry Ford's day. Only now, to win in the battle for customers, you will need to do more than sharpen your focus. You will need to deliver on your claims continuously and convince your customers that you have done exactly that every single year when you re-apply for the business you won just twelve months before.

This leads to the central thesis of this book: The ability to succeed in this new economy will depend on how well you sell and deliver measurable business outcomes to your customers. Indeed, we believe that constantly demonstrating delivery of customer value may be one of the few ways companies can attract and retain customers over the long-term. Gone are the days of sustainable competitive advantage. If you're not generating tangible value for customers, you're at risk of losing them.

Are your customers truly benefiting from your products and services? Are you doing enough to ensure your customers are successful? Can you measure what success looks like for them? These are questions we believe must be top of mind for business leaders today.

The answers to these questions will be different for each company. Underneath these differences, however, is a set of core customer-centric principles and practices that we believe apply across every business organization. These principles comprise a critical new capability we call "customer success delivery."

Specifically, we define customer success delivery as a disciplined way of making your customers' success and measurable business outcomes part of your corporate DNA. In our view, every function in your organization that impacts the customer—including but not limited to sales, marketing, service, support, and engineering—must make customer success a central tenet of their charters. And they must do it together. Five separate customer success strategies will not yield results.

The Three Pillars of Customer Success

Our goal is to provide business leaders with a practical guidebook including proven practices for making customer success a core part of your organizational DNA. In the chapters ahead, we'll explore three critical capabilities—or pillars—that we think are absolutely essential to prospering in what market researcher Forrester calls the Age of the Customer.[2] These are the pillars:

- **Listening.** Learn how to be completely plugged in to your customers and understand exactly what they need, how their needs evolve, and what it means for them to be successful with your products.

- **Engaging.** Find out how to start a productive dialog with customers, collaboratively solve problems, and embed yourself into your customer's business.

- **Ensuring.** Promote customer loyalty with innovative strategies and techniques that help you deliver on your promises and increase the likelihood that your customers realize the value expected from using your products.

For each pillar, we offer a real-life case study of an organization that excels in one or more of these capabilities. Some have restored trust frayed from years of neglect, fueling new sales. Others have leveraged feedback from customers to design enormously successful new products.

To be clear, we're not recommending that you abandon your existing customer-oriented efforts, such as your loyalty programs, your "net promoter" scoring systems, or the like. Rather, we are advocating that you make a serious effort at understanding and measuring how much value your customers are currently realizing from your products and services, and take concrete steps to enable them to reach full potential. If that means integrating these principles into existing customer programs or creating a separate customer success organization, that is something business leaders must figure out for themselves in the context of their organization's unique culture and market environment.

Outcomes First

Our approach stands out from other frameworks for understanding customer relationships in one significant way: It puts *business outcomes* front and center in how you market, sell, support, and create products for customers.

In *Competing for Customers,* we blend insights from top experts with our own firsthand experience in industries ranging from high technology to retail. Each of us brings a unique perspective to the subject—and we also hold some pretty strong convictions formed over decades of working with customers inside leading global companies. Jeb Dasteel is chief customer officer of Oracle, one of the world's largest providers of business software and hardware. Amir Hartman is the best-selling author of the Ruthless Execution series and the book

Net Ready; former faculty member of the University of California, Berkeley's Haas School of Business; and co-founder of Mainstay, a leading Silicon Valley consulting firm. Craig LeGrande, co-founder of Mainstay, co-author of *Ruthless Execution II,* and author of numerous industry strategy papers for top technology firms, has more than two decades of management consulting experience for Fortune 500 clients.

All of us share a passion for understanding customer relationships. We've made careers out of figuring out what drives customer behavior: what attracts customers to vendors, what makes them buy, and what sustains their loyalty over time.

We'd love to hear what you think about the ideas we lay out in this book. Please share your thoughts by going to our website www.competingforcustomers.com, where you can also sign up for our *Competing for Customers* e-mail newsletter.

Endnotes

[1] Cited in CMSWire.com, "The Internet of Things Will Change Everything, Including the Economy," Nov 2013, comments made by Gartner Research at the Gartner Symposium ITXPO 2013.

[2] Forrester Research (https://www.forrester.com/age-of-the-customer/-/E-MPL291).

1

Two Meta Trends Shaping the Competition

"A business absolutely devoted to service will have only one worry about profits. They will be embarrassingly large."

–Henry Ford

Though it may seem like an old-school truism, it has taken businesses quite a long time to realize the importance of "putting customers first." But they are starting to finally get it. Indeed, as we'll explain shortly, they may have no other choice if they expect to survive the onslaught of two "meta trends" we describe in this chapter.

Over the years a lot of companies have spent significant sums in their effort to understand their customers. Many were inspired by the ideas of Don Peppers and Martha Rogers, whose groundbreaking book, *The One to One Future,*[1] introduced the world to the concept of customer relationship management.

Peppers and Rogers were followed by authors like Frederick Reichheld of Bain & Company, whose seminal works *The Loyalty Effect* and *The Ultimate Question* introduced now-standard concepts such as customer loyalty, and promoted creative strategies for retaining customers.

Although these pioneering works provided motivation for a generation of business leaders to turn their attention squarely on the customer, we propose that companies today will need to do even more—indeed, to think about customers in an entirely new way—if they expect to reap Henry Ford's supersized profits.

That new way of thinking about the customer is embodied in a set of principles and techniques we call customer success delivery. Specifically, we define customer success delivery as the ability to quantify and communicate the value of your product or service consistently and continuously, from before the sale to long after, while measuring and delivering on the promise of enabling business outcomes.

Why is mastering the art of customer success delivery so important and so urgent? Simply speaking, it's because we believe it will be an indispensable capability for thriving in the face of two meta trends of the next decade: the Customer First Revolution and the Subscription Economy. In this chapter, we will explore both of these uber-trends—along with a handful of derivative movements—that are rapidly defining the competitive landscape for the near- to mid-term future.

Growing Gap

The gap between today's business activities and reaching the goals of customer success remains large. According to recent research from Peppers & Rogers,[2]

- 48% of respondents (out of more than 100 enterprise business decision makers, 2012) stated they had not made any attempts to correlate customer experience (success) with business performance outcomes.

- 41% stated they are currently examining correlations between customer experience and business performance outcomes (e.g., shareholder value, revenue generation, customer acquisition).

- Less than 10% carefully monitor and act on customer experience information gathered across all touch points.

> • Only 39% of respondents said that they are achieving the kind of progress they expected due to issues such as siloed data across functions and channels.

To better serve their customers, more companies are forming teams specifically focused on driving customer success. Signaling the strategic importance of the effort, companies are now placing these teams under the direction of top-level company leadership. A great example is Oracle's customer success program guided by our co-author Jeb Dasteel, Oracle chief customer officer.

Meta Trend #1: The Customer First Revolution

As the title of this book suggests, we're in the midst of a revolution—one that is shaping up to be one of the biggest forces influencing how you compete for customers—indeed, how you run your whole business—over the next decade. We call it the Customer First Revolution.

If you're an earlier-generation business, the Customer First Revolution changes the rules of the game completely. Sure, you've always wanted to nurture great relationships with customers, but at the end of the day, you've always been the one who sets the terms of the sale and the direction of the relationship. What the revolution decrees is the opposite: Now (for reasons we'll explain below), it's the customer who sets the rules of engagement. In other words, after decades of subservience to the seller, the customer has finally become the proverbial king!

Customer First Companies Perform Better

Business-to-consumer (B2C) companies were the first to see the tables turning when social media and other digital channels burst onto the scene a decade ago. These new tools and tactics, which customers eagerly adopted as a means to level the playing field against sellers, forced B2C companies to radically rethink their marketing and sales strategies.

Market analyst Forrester Research, which coined the term "the Age of the Customer" to describe our revolutionary era, discovered an interesting fact about this trend: B2C companies that learned to embrace these next-generation tactics—and used them to improve the customer experience—gained a dramatic performance edge over those that didn't. Indeed, they outperformed the average company by a considerable margin and outperformed laggards by more than a factor of three (see Figure 1.1).

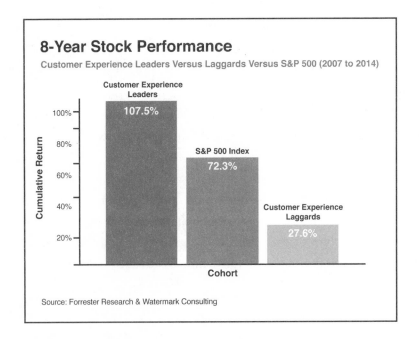

Figure 1.1 Customer First companies outperform the rest.

Mastering Your Digital Identity Is Critical

The Customer First Revolution puts a premium on all things digital, and for good reason: Increasingly, your customers are digital animals, and they increasingly relate to your business and brand on a digital terrain. It's no exaggeration to say that your customer to a large extent *defines* your brand through digital vehicles and channels such as Facebook, Foursquare, Twitter, LinkedIn—the list grows longer every day.

It is now estimated that some 15 million consumers engage with their brands through social media before making a buying decision. And that number is fast-growing, with B2B customers trending similarly.[3]

In the digital- and social-powered Customer First Revolution, consumers will interact with your digital identity even before visiting your brick-and-mortar location. It is also a world where relevance and authenticity trump prepackaged, one-size-fits-all content. Companies that master the art of creating and managing a compelling digital identity will have the upper hand in the Customer First Revolution.

Local Beats Corporate

Delivering relevance and authenticity will mean that it's not enough to have a slick corporate website. In the Customer First Revolution, your *local* digital identity matters more. That refers to all the social media activities and chatter tied to your neighborhood stores, franchises, and branches—the places where your customers shop, eat, and hang out.[4] This is where opinions about your brand are formed, and then shared far and wide over the digital airwaves. Nowadays, before you dine out—or sign up for a health club—chances are you'll check the customer reviews on social media and get directions while you're at it.

So crucial is this local angle that we're seeing a new discipline emerging around managing a company's local digital presence, or "digital place identity." And it is serious business. We recently talked to a national restaurant chain that initially failed to pay attention to the Facebook pages of its local eateries. As a result, it left a digital brand vacuum that was filled by "rogue" pages filled with a hodge-podge of negative and even false reviews cooked up anonymously. Its digital brand had been hijacked, and sales suffered for months.

Going Local Pays

In a pilot program, a national restaurant chain recently compared the performance of locally targeted Facebook content against a control group without any managed local social presence and found significant improvements, including the following:

- 650,000 unique local customers reached
- 7,200 net gain in transactions
- 7.1% net increase in revenue
- 30x higher return on investment

B2B Customers Are Seizing Power

Although consumer-focused companies were the first to be swept up in the Customer First Revolution, we're now seeing this same shift in power spreading into the business-to-business (B2B) universe. And we are seeing the same advantages accrue to B2B companies that embrace the shift to customers' digital experiences—for example, by launching social channels targeting key customer segments. Parallels to the consumer sector abound, though with some subtle differences. Instead of Facebook or Yelp, for example, business buyers prefer B2B-oriented channels such as LinkedIn and IT Central Station.

Buying Happens Even Before the First Phone Call

The revolution is leading more B2B buyers to shun vendor sales reps in favor of company and independent websites. In a recent survey by Forrester Research, B2B buyers said by a margin of three to one that gathering information online is actually superior to interacting with a sales rep. Furthermore, these same buyers said by a margin of 59% to 19% they did not want to interact with sales reps as their primary source of information.[5] Three quarters of B2B buyers in another Forrester survey said they researched half or more of their work purchases online, with the top source of this research being vendor websites.[6]

With the lion's share of research being done online, it's estimated that 70% or more of the buying decision happens *before* the company is contacted directly. Armed with intelligence and candid insights gleaned from social media, the Internet, and analyst research, business decision makers are more likely to home in on one or two providers that can meet their needs. This makes it even more important for sellers to develop a compelling value proposition and disseminate it strategically across digital and social media networks.

Meta Trend #2: The Subscription Economy

Why own when you can rent? That's the sentiment of more and more businesses these days when it comes to acquiring everything from the software that runs your company to the boost in power you need from your wind farm. We believe this shift in mind-set and buying habits represents nothing short of a sea change in the structure of the modern economy, and we rank it alongside the Customer First Revolution as one of the two meta trends that businesses must come to grips with in the coming decade.

We define the Subscription Economy as the fundamental transformation from an economy based on high capital-intensive sales of *products* into an economy based on *services* that you pay for as you use them, or as specific outcomes are realized.

The Subscription Economy, as a pervasive phenomenon, is still in the early innings, but its growth is visible all around us and massive disruptions are sweeping through key industries from high tech to transportation to manufacturing. One of the best-known examples is the software industry, which is currently witnessing a major shift from packaged software to "cloud subscriptions."

If you intend to win the competition for customers, you would be smart to understand why businesses are flocking to the subscription model of doing business, and begin to think creatively about how you can make your own business "subscription friendly."

The "Cloudification" of Business

A key driver of the Subscription Economy is a critical new business capability we call the "cloudification" of business—a term coined in the book, *Ruthless Execution, Second Edition.* What does it mean to "cloudify" your business? It means digitizing your products and services and transforming them into an offering—or platform—that is accessed over the Internet. In some cases companies establish a marketplace by "opening up" their product, turning it into a broad platform on which others can add value and new offerings.[7] Cloudifying your business provides a new way to stay closer to your customer. It has clearly become the third wave of the Internet revolution, in which products and services are put on the cloud for customers to use as needed.

Investment Equations Will Be Radically Realigned

The significance of the cloudification of business is far-reaching and anything but trivial, since many established business models and partnerships will be rendered obsolete. First, it radically changes the investment equation for customers by lowering up-front capital requirements. This has the advantage of better aligning the customer's investment with the returns. Instead of paying for most of the investment up-front in the hope that it will pay off down the road, now your customer's investment costs are spread over the life of the solution and are more in line with the incremental benefits they see from your solution year to year.

Switching Costs Don't Matter Anymore

One of the strongest attractions of the Subscription Economy is this: If you ever find you're not seeing enough benefit compared to what you're paying, it's relatively easy to "unsubscribe" and shop for a new service. What this means is that across many industries a long-standing strategic force and pillar of protection—switching costs—is being marginalized. We're not suggesting that switching costs are dead. In industries where large and expensive physical assets are involved, switching costs will still be relevant; however, the influence to shape vendor performance and expected business outcomes will significantly increase for customers. Increasingly, industry leaders will need to design new incentives for staying—such as providing a clearly superior customer experience—but the cost or hassle of switching won't be one of them. Instead, companies will need to develop an ongoing stream of new capabilities to deliver value.

Barriers to Entry Will Crumble

Just as the barriers to customer defection are eroding, so too are the traditional obstacles to competitors invading your turf or creating a whole new market seemingly out of nowhere. A great example is Amazon. The Seattle-based behemoth started off as a bookseller before extending its web platform to include just about anything you wanted to buy on the planet. Then in 2003, while retooling its data centers to improve its Web application, Amazon discovered it could take some of the computing power in the revamped centers and "rent it out" through the cloud.

Practically overnight, Amazon Web Services (AWS) was born, and it swiftly skyrocketed to become one of the biggest forces in cloud services. Netflix, to take one example, now runs its streaming video services over bandwidth it rents from AWS. *Forbes* magazine recently declared AWS the "largest pubic cloud vendor on earth,"[8] leaving entrenched computing giants like IBM, Oracle, and Microsoft scrambling to catch up. In the Subscription Economy, traditional barriers that incumbents depended on to fend off upstarts have melted away.

Products Will Morph into Services

The spreading Subscription Economy will see more products being refashioned as services. Just "taking delivery" of equipment is no longer good enough for customers who increasingly prefer to shift the headache and risk of maintenance and breakdowns to the vendor. That's why companies like Rockwell Automation—profiled in Chapter 9, "How Rockwell Automation Measures Success"—are reinventing their factory automation products, incorporating Internet of Things technologies so that assembly-line machines can monitor themselves, self-install new software, and preempt breakdowns without ever bothering the customer. It is a far more servicelike experience, saves time and money, and also manages to create a new kind of "stickiness" that dissuades customers from straying to the competition.

A different example is Cisco, which has been the dominant player in the computer networking industry for the past two decades. For years the company's primary source of revenue had been physical gear like routers and switches that companies install in their data centers. But with more customers preferring to rent computing power, Cisco has begun offering the equivalent of "networking as a service" in which Cisco owns the networking infrastructure, monitors its performance, upgrades it, and adds bandwidth as needed—all from a remote command center. Cisco expects this portion of its revenue stream to continue to grow over the next decade, perhaps soon rivaling its traditional hardware sales.

Delivering Outcomes Will Be Critical

The Subscription Economy, with its "what have you done for me lately" culture, will shine a harsh light on business outcomes. Is your customer able to reduce costs as promised? Get more output out of your machines? Cut downtime as expected? Drive new revenue? The new "as a service" economy puts less emphasis on the particular product you're pedaling and more on what it can do for your customers. Increasingly, your customers don't care about your products, but about the business outcomes that matter most to them. That's why the most innovative enterprises on the planet are focusing on selling and delivering business outcomes. We'll profile several of these outcomes-centric companies in the pages ahead.

Why Customers Love to Subscribe

The Subscription Economy gives customers key advantages over traditional investment scenarios:

- **Minimal upfront capital requirements.** Companies typically treat subscription costs as an ongoing operating expense, and often pay only for as much as they use.

- **Hold vendors' feet to the fire.** Since customers pay as they go and can switch with relative ease, they're in a strong position to demand the most from vendors.

- **One throat to choke.** Subscriptions typically come with all the supporting services bundled in a turnkey package provided by a single company. That means just one vendor to hold accountable.

- **Focus on what matters.** Subscribing to a service frequently allows companies to offload the burden of managing a complex operation, letting them specialize in their areas of competitive advantage.

- **New features continuously delivered.** Cloud providers have universally adopted a strategy of continuously delivering new features, or capabilities, throughout the life of the subscription.

The emerging Subscription Economy and Customer First Revolution will force businesses to take a hard look at how they are currently doing sales, marketing, product development, services, and support. In many cases, long-standing processes will need to be reorganized and transformed. For example:

- Sales teams will need to shift some of their focus from inking a deal to proving *business value* to customers. Doing this early on will open up opportunities for additional sales. Teams will need to remain vigilant year-round, especially as renewals loom, and be prepared to show continuing value delivery to minimize churn.

- In a similar fashion, marketing groups will need to reorient their campaigns around longer-term relationships that require constant nurturing to avoid defections. So marketing becomes less about nurturing leads and more about nurturing relationships. And companies will need to market the advantages of "maturing" with their solutions.

- Professional services and product development teams will see dramatic changes as well, with a new emphasis on collaboration with customers and business results.

- Operations and support teams will need to be more proactive than ever before, constantly monitoring key performance data and using predictive analytics and possibly embedded sensors to ensure that the solution is meeting expectations.

Is your business ready to take on the Customer First Revolution? To thrive in the Subscription Economy? In the next chapter, we'll share with you three key capabilities that we believe are essential to succeeding in the new customer-centric, outcomes-focused, subscription-powered world. These include new skills and processes for *listening* to your customers to uncover what matters to them; *engaging* them creatively and authentically to build credibility and loyalty; and finally *ensuring* that the outcomes you promise are fulfilled—perhaps the most critical but also the most difficult skill to master. Across each of these areas, we will also stress the importance of *measuring* to accurately define your customer's challenges and the value you're delivering.

Overcoming Barriers to Success

As the two significant waves of change described in this chapter—the Customer First Revolution and the rise of subscription business models—continue to make their way through the economy, some companies will flourish and others will struggle. To succeed, companies must overcome the following challenges:

Challenge #1: Breaking Down Information Silos

Many B2B firms are still too compartmentalized and lack efficient systems for sharing information *across* departments and with outside partners. This frequently leads to embarrassing knowledge gaps and crossed wires, with customer relationships invariably suffering. Customer executives complain about mixed sales messages; internal disagreements; frustrated channel partners; and even internal competition surfacing in front of the customer. As you take stock of your business communications infrastructure, consider looking at technology solutions that compile multiple streams of customer data and can serve as an early warning system to spot customer attrition as well as sales opportunities.

Challenge #2: Bucking Old Marketing Habits

Marketing and sales teams still focus too much on hyping features and functions of products, and not enough on what customers want the products to deliver in terms of business outcomes. Common bad habits include producing too much marketing fluff, creating content that is too technical, and failing to paint the bigger picture for customers. For example, a university looking to build a "classroom of the future" isn't interested just in purchasing video equipment but in linking video to other classroom technologies such as digital whiteboards, learning management systems, and desktop apps in the cloud. Make a conscious effort to position your company not merely as a practical tool but as a strategic enabler in a larger world.

Challenge #3: Thinking Beyond the Transaction

Companies continue to remain too focused on closing the deal instead of helping customers realize the business value promised.

To make the sale, companies will often marshal a parade of experts from engineers to executives, only to move them over to the next deal after the contract is signed. Such transitory deal focus is myopic and can lead to poor results, including higher service costs, greater churn rates, and a tarnished brand. Few companies realize the full potential value of technology investments. Increase the odds of better results by structuring sales engagements to ensure that teams stay connected to the customer well after the ink dries on the contract.

Challenge #4: Building an Effective Ecosystem

You might say it takes a village to ensure customer success. The reality is that the ability to assemble an efficient and motivated network of go-to-market partners is key to providing a complete array of auxiliary products and services that customers need in order to cover all the bases in a growing global marketplace. New automated third-party management platforms can streamline your partner ecosystem and reduce common compliance and performance risks.

Challenge #5: Delving Deeper Than Customer Surveys

Most customer experience and success programs focus on assessing the happiness or satisfaction level of a customer. That's a necessary first step, but surveys rarely provide a complete picture of the customer experience, a gap that can come back to bite you. The fact is, most surveys only reveal overall customer sentiment and technical problems with your product, and they generally miss deeper issues like a faulty licensing model or poor ROI. This shortcoming could be corrected—and customer leakage prevented—by a more sophisticated customer feedback program and investing in business case and benefits realization capabilities. Furthermore, it's to your advantage to build systems now that can collect, analyze, and react to the growing flow of customer service and product performance data that will become available as the Internet of Things continues to gain traction.

Endnotes

[1] *The One to One Future,* Don Peppers and Martha Rogers, Crown Business, 1993.

[2] "The ROI of Customer Experience: A New Economy Approach to Growth and Profitability," Peppers & Rogers Group, Teletech, 2012.

[3] "Social Media: You'll Like This," CPCU Society, 2014.

[4] In fact, our research found that an estimated 40% of national brands have unauthorized duplicates of their locations on Facebook and Foursquare.

[5] "Death of a B2B Salesman," Forrester Research, Andy Hoar, April 2015.

[6] "B2B Marketers Can Govern L2RM with the Funnel but Must Design to the Customer Life Cycle," Forrester Research, Lori Wizdo, March 2015.

[7] Excerpt from *Ruthless Execution: How Business Leaders Manage Through Turbulent Times, Second Edition,* iBooks.

[8] *Forbes Magazine,* May 2015.

2

Making the Case for Customer Success

"There is only one boss. The customer. And he can fire every-body in the company from the chairman on down, simply by spending his money somewhere else."

—Sam Walton

In the preceding chapter, we described two meta trends that are shaping the new economy—namely, the Customer First Revolution and the Subscription Economy. We argued that to stay ahead of these trends—indeed, to harness them—business will need to embrace a radically new way of thinking about customers, one informed by a set of principles and techniques we call customer success delivery.

We define customer success delivery as the ability to develop and deploy business practices that target, track, and measure customer success with the goal of helping customers achieve desired business outcomes. We believe that by transforming your business to capture and promote your customers' success objectives, you can thrive in this new environment. We start with a discussion of the strategic reasons to move to a customer success-focused business model.

Managing in an Upside-Down World

The spread of the Subscription Economy will have huge consequences for B2B businesses in virtually every industry, upending traditional revenue models that companies have operated with for decades. Here's the difference: In the "old world," business buyers spent the majority of their investment dollars up front—typically upon signing the deal—but these buyers wouldn't see the benefit of that investment until years down the road, if at all. The customer therefore bore the lion's share of the risk of any given investment and could only *hope* that the costs it sunk into the purchase would pay off over time.

In the Subscription Economy, however, this conventional risk equation is changing. Customers now have more choices, including how they buy, deploy, and manage business solutions. In the "new world," revenue and risk models are being turned upside down, with customers spending less up front and bearing far less risk that a given investment will fail to deliver business value. Figure 2.1 depicts this new reality.

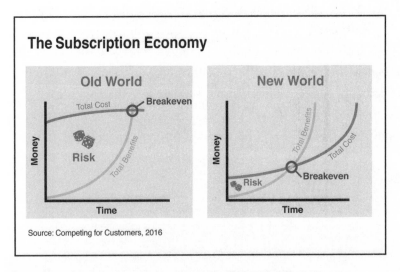

Figure 2.1 Advantage customer: less risk, faster payoffs in the new Subscription Economy.

We believe there are five key economic drivers that will impact B2B revenue streams and business priorities in the emerging Subscription Economy:

- **More revenue will be delayed.** As increasing numbers of customers pay as they go, more revenue will be delayed and spread over time. To take an example from the software industry: In the past, a typical purchase might have consisted of a several-million-dollar software license deal, which customers paid up front and treated as a capital expenditure (CAPEX). In the Subscription Economy, however, that same customer may spend only a fraction of that sum initially, paying instead for "software as a service" on a monthly (or yearly) basis according to the number of people or "seats" using the software. It's not unreasonable to expect that the several million dollars would be spread over three years.

- **Revenue growth will require more engagement.** If vendors hope to grow near-term subscription revenue by implementing the solution in more locations or by adding more users, they will need to engage with the customer continuously after the sale and be vigilant about communicating the success of the solution.

- **To prevent early switching, rapid value delivery will be required.** With reduced risk, more customers will take advantage of pay-as-you-go arrangements to test or "trial run" products, while keeping competing products in mind as an option should they become dissatisfied. This will force sellers to *deliver value quickly*—and communicate that success early and often—to keep customers committed.

- **To sustain revenue, ongoing innovation will be expected.** Customers expect subscription services to improve over time as technical and business-process innovations are constantly incorporated into the service. If vendors can't meet the customers' innovation expectations, future revenues are put at risk. The norm in a subscription environment is to expect value-creating updates to the service multiple times a year.

- **Delivering fast break-even results will be key.** One of the most important milestones for the customer is the break-even point—when benefits realized equal the amount invested. In the subscription model, customer spending will spread out to more effectively tie incremental customer investments to incremental business outcomes. Companies must ensure speed-to-value to capture and retain revenue.

In short, the upside-down world of subscription revenue compels business leaders to reorder their priorities, focusing less attention on *acquiring* customers and more on keeping the ones they have happy—both immediately after the sale and over the long haul. Thus, it's imperative for companies to have a well-thought-out retention strategy as part of their blueprint for ensuring customer success.

First-Mover Advantage

Companies shouldn't wait to launch a customer success strategy, even if it's not a perfect one. There are distinct advantages to being early to market with a customer success program. First, you'll avoid being "crowded out" by competitors who are vying with you for the limited attention span of business buyers. A good comparison is the dot.com land grab of the early 2000s, which saw latecomers—even those with better products—pushed off the stage by first movers.

Moreover, by showing early on that you're capable of helping drive innovation in your customer's industry—which we believe should be a core component of your customer success strategy—you'll erect a valuable switching barrier, a rare edge in an economy in which such impediments have all but disappeared. Demonstrating a willingness to "co-invest" in products and research to give your customers a competitive edge is another strategy that, if launched earlier rather than later in the relationship, can help you secure business for years.

Snowball Effect

Another advantage of building a customer success capability is the *recursive* nature of relationship-building activities. By this we mean that each activity you engage in feeds and builds upon the other, making each iteration of your customer success program more effective and powerful. Consider the following example:

> *Step 1.* A company sets up a listening post—let's say an executive breakfast with insurance company CIOs. The meeting results in a lively discussion about how to keep customer data safe.

> *Step 2.* The discussion spurs the company to tee up new research to communicate the company's secure, industry-specialized customer data management practices; this leads to a whitepaper and sales collateral.

> *Step 3.* That effort fuels additional customer engagement activities, including an executive briefing, creating a security assessment tool, and drawing up a business case template used by salespeople to communicate the company's unique approach.

> *Step 4.* Results of the business case, measured by the vendor's post-sales audit, are then funneled back to the marketing group. These results form the basis of a success story, benchmarks for the next business case, and an industry executive briefing as described in step 1—driving another round of customer engagement.

This example illustrates the goal of our book: to provide business leaders with a blueprint for making customer success delivery part of their organizational DNA. It is about helping B2B companies develop an innate capacity to ensure that customers are achieving the business outcomes that matter to them. This focus on outcomes and results distinguishes our customer success approach with other strategies that emphasize customer centricity, satisfaction, and loyalty. We believe that if you put delivering business outcomes at the center of your customer relationships, you'll be in the best position to succeed in the emerging customer-first Subscription Economy.

The Economic Justification for Customer Success Delivery

There are compelling economic reasons for adopting a business model aligned with customer success. For example, research has long shown that it can cost three to six times more to attract new customers than it does to keep an existing customer.[1] As we'll detail in this chapter, B2B vendors will face rising cash flow pressures unless they make sustained efforts at retaining customers. In other words, companies that institutionalize customer success programs and make the attainment of customer business outcomes part of their DNA will stand to benefit significantly. The benefits include both stronger revenue growth and bigger profit margins.

Specifically, a well-executed customer success business model can help companies drive revenue and profit in three ways:

1. By *preserving existing revenue* through reducing customer churn

2. By *expanding existing revenue* through enhanced up-selling and cross-selling

3. By *generating new revenue* through customer referrals

Figure 2.2 illustrates how benefits can be derived from lower customer churn, upselling and cross-selling, lower acquisition costs, sales acceleration, and a lower cost of sales.

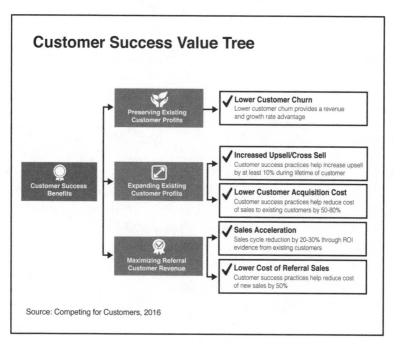

Figure 2.2 Customer success revenue impact.

Protecting Revenue

B2B companies can preserve revenue streams first and foremost by holding onto existing customers—that is, by reducing "churn"—and the best way to do this is by implementing smart means for assuring and promoting customer success. Particularly in subscription businesses, these will include programs and resources that:

1. Assess how customers measure success.

2. Ensure optimal product usage.

3. Track whether that usage ties directly to customer business outcomes.

4. Quantify those outcomes in terms that relate to how customers measure success.

The Compounding Power of Customer Retention

Reducing churn to a minimum can have powerful repercussions over time, similar to compound interest. In fact, according to analyst Mikael Blaisdell, customer retention rates approaching 95% can *double* the valuation of a company compared to an 80% rate. As seen in Figure 2.3, high customer churn acts like a negative interest rate, compounding lost revenue year after year and ultimately putting the brakes on business growth. Companies that are able to reduce churn by 5%, for example, typically see a 20% increase in revenue over five years.[2]

Furthermore, our research[3] indicates that companies can reduce their customer churn rate to about 2% to 3% (from the average 10% to 20%) by proactively managing post-purchase customer experience and increasing the likelihood that customers will achieve favorable business outcomes.

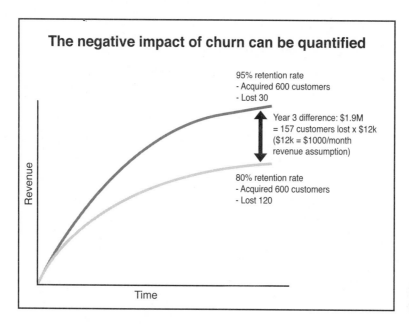

Figure 2.3 Reduction in churn economic impact example.

Although companies will always need to acquire *net-new* customers to fuel growth, the largest share of revenue and profit improvement will continue to come from the existing customer base. In fact, for businesses based mostly on recurring revenue, almost *all* the profit will come from their "installed base." Indeed, often as much as 80% of the total revenue required to turn a subscription-based profit isn't collected until long after the sale is closed and the customer has "re-upped" to extend the contract. This is in stark contrast to the traditional up-front capital-purchase scenario, in which as much as 60% of total lifetime revenue is collected upon signing of the contract.

For the Subscription Economy companies that we studied, it took at least three years to accumulate the same amount of revenue that had been collected up front in the traditional CAPEX model. However, even though a significant portion of revenue was delayed, profits rose because the overall relationship was *strengthened and lengthened*. This is due to the introduction of customer success practices such as listening posts, strategic engagement programs, and adoption strategies that we'll focus on in the coming chapters.

To reduce churn, companies can start by hiring customer success managers tasked with gauging product usage and satisfaction levels and proactively working to avert dropouts through proactive engagement strategies and early intervention. Such efforts not only reduce customer churn but also shave costs by avoiding expensive last-ditch remediation or retention campaigns. In fact, in one of our recent studies, we discovered that companies employing customer success programs and tools to detect customer issues early spent 80% less on retaining customers. Imagine, what would your business look like if you dramatically increased the retention of your customers? Or even just reduced churn by half?

Beyond Management by Expiration Date

Customer churn was a big issue at a certain software company that works with businesses to discover sales opportunities and grow revenue. Executives admitted that customer retention mainly involved "management by expiration date"—or simply waiting for the contract renewal date to approach before starting retention activities. That was before it started tracking usage of its products through a cloud-based customer success management platform and tying that data to its customer relationship management system. Now it's seeing customer warning signs—as well as up-selling opportunities—60 days earlier. Churn is starting to fall, with up-sell and cross-sell revenue on track for a 10% lift.

Expanding Revenue by Building on Your Base

Being proactive about customer success is a great way to reduce churn and keep your revenue stream from ebbing. It's also one of the most potent ways to actively *grow* revenue because it allows you to sell more to your existing customers. Of course, selling to current customers has always been easier than bringing new customers onboard. According to Market Metrics, the probability of selling to an existing customer is 60% to 70%, whereas selling to a new prospect ranges from 5% to 20%.[4] However, this insider edge can easily vanish if you drop the ball with your existing base and ignore what's driving their business. Without an active effort at promoting customer success, the likelihood your customers will buy again from you falls significantly.

This is why up-selling and cross-selling success rises significantly at companies that consistently employ customer success practices such as proactive listening posts, strategic engagement programs, and outcomes-focused commercial models. The resulting flood of insights helps marketing and sales teams identify add-on products and services that make sense for individual customers. Moreover, customer success-oriented programs fuel productive fact-based conversations that continue to bear fruit throughout the customer lifecycle.

For example, if you've set up systems for collecting and tracking your customers' product adoption data, you now have a powerful set of facts at your disposal to argue for an even broader rollout (to more employees, other business units, or added geographic regions) or for incorporating complementary products and services to create more value. Behind the scenes, this same usage data can help you devise marketing campaigns and sales strategies that are grounded in reality.

Recent data shows that customer success-driven up-selling can boost revenue by 10% or more.[5] To be sure, each company will benefit in different ways, depending on its size, industry, customer spending patterns, number of customers, and so on. However, research is now showing that companies that actively manage customer success and experience may see a two- to threefold increase in up-sell revenue over less effective peers.[6]

Extending Revenue with Referrals

We've shown how customer success delivery can strengthen your core revenue stream by reducing churn and convincing your customer base to buy more. But remember that successful customers are also more likely to serve as advocates for your products and services, sending you first-time customers on the strength of their referrals, word of mouth, social media sharing, and more. It's like hiring an unpaid virtual sales force.

There's little doubt that when your customers have a truly great onboarding experience and are hitting milestones and achieving business outcomes—which is precisely what effective customer success delivery is designed to provide—they will be far more likely to recommend your products and services. And when you supplement advocacy activities with other customer success practices, such as providing quantifiable customer proof points and evidence-based investment justification, you can reduce the sales cycle by as much as 30% to 40%.[7]

What's more, referred customers cost less to acquire. Research from Satmetrix indicates that the cost to acquire a new customer referred by an advocate is 50% lower than a non-referred customer.[8]

Because Satmetrix estimates that B2B companies have an average of about 10% to 20% "strong advocates," one can easily imagine the growth potential and cost advantages of using customer success programs to recruit more advocates. In fact, we believe such sales-boosting referral programs could easily become one of the most significant growth platforms of the next decade.

Do You Really Care About Customer Success?

Do you really care? Of course you do. Every B2B business leader we talk to tells us their company is trying to help customers be successful in achieving their goals. But when asked to describe specific initiatives they've launched to that end, leaders either point to their customer service and support operations, or look at us with a blank stare.

In researching this book, we asked more than a hundred B2B executives about their companies' customer success programs and practices. Then we posed some of the same questions to their customers. As shown in Figure 2.4, the difference between how sellers and buyers perceived the relationship was surprisingly large, exceeding 50% in most cases, with sellers consistently overestimating the closeness and effectiveness of the relationship. Indeed, we've found the perception among B2B executives that their business is "almost there" to be pervasive today, when in fact most still have a long way to go. What the gap points to is the need for B2B companies to make significant investments in customer success capabilities.

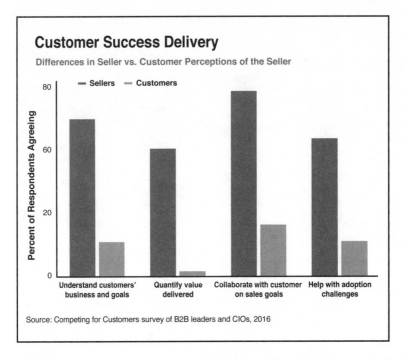

Figure 2.4 Contrasting views: how B2B sellers and customers perceive their relationship.

The Customer Success Investment Landscape

Thus far we've outlined the new revenue economics that are spurring companies to adopt customer success delivery as a core business strategy. We've highlighted the salient features of this new business landscape, including the role reversal in which customers increasingly will expect sellers to take on more risk in the relationship. The upside for B2B vendors who can effectively navigate the new landscape is huge. It includes not only a short-term revenue lift from existing customers, but a rising tide of value stretching over the lifetime of the customer relationship.

Competing successfully in this mostly uncharted territory, we argue, will depend on your ability to deliver business outcomes that matter to your customers. Simply stated, customer success must become part of your organizational DNA and should factor into every interaction you have with customers, every product and service you develop, and the operation of every department in your organization.

Achieving the benefits outlined previously will require a broad and well-coordinated effort and most likely significant business investments, although we'll outline easy ways to get started in the chapters ahead. Figure 2.5 summarizes some of the key investments companies should consider when moving to a customer success business model.

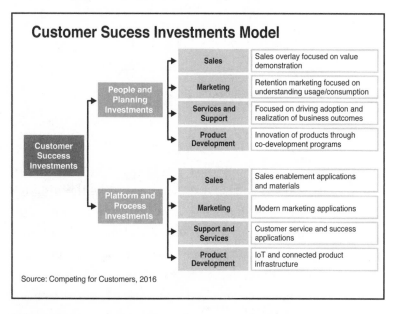

Figure 2.5 Customer success business investments.

The Three Pillars of Customer Success

In researching this book, we saw companies employing hundreds of strategies, techniques, and technologies in an effort to understand

and deliver success for their customers. As highlighted in Figure 2.6, *Competing for Customers* has grouped these capabilities into three *customer success pillars:* listening, engaging, and ensuring.

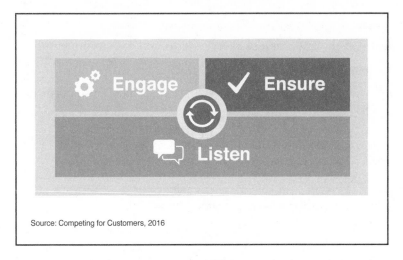

Source: Competing for Customers, 2016

Figure 2.6 The three pillars of customer success.

- **Listening.** This capability is about understanding your customers' needs and goals, monitoring how effectively customers are using your products and services, and measuring the resulting business impact. The best companies invest in listening programs and technologies that continuously monitor customer opinion, analyze feedback from key stakeholders and users, and even "listen in" on the product itself while it's being used. Listening methods include both "old school" surveys, focus groups, and the like and "new school" listening posts such as social media, listening features built into business applications, and connected smart machines. Chapters 3, "Listen," and 4, "Telogis Listens for Success," shed more light on this critical capability.

- **Engaging.** This capability refers to building a trusted advisor relationship with your customers. It's about creatively interacting with your customers to learn what *their* top priorities are, how *their* performance is measured, and in turn coming up with innovative solutions and visionary capabilities that allow *their* businesses to succeed and innovate. This takes thought leadership, including value-based communications to key customer stakeholders in a language that they care about. Chapters 5, "Engage," and 6, "Cisco: Engaging Customers to Deliver Business Outcomes," delve deeper into the topic of strategic engagement.

- **Ensuring.** This capability involves making sure your customers are successfully implementing, adopting, and realizing the full potential of what you've sold them. Often this entails taking action to help drive product adoption and consumption to increase the likelihood of the desired business outcomes and then presenting those achievements to customer leadership. In some cases, as we'll see in Chapter 7, "Ensure," 8, "How GE Power Fuels Growth by Delivering Outcomes," and 9, "How Rockwell Automation Measures Success," vendors are actually selling *business outcomes* rather than the products and services themselves.

Needless to say, acquiring these capabilities won't be a simple task for most companies. Odds are, they'll need to reinvent, reposition, and modernize crucial functions and processes across the business, including sales, marketing, product development, services, and support. In Chapters 10, "Creating a Blueprint for Customer Success," and 11, "How Oracle Focuses on Customer Success," we'll explore how adopting a customer success-centric business model can impact these core functions throughout the customer lifecycle. For now, let's dig deeper into the first of the three critical capabilities necessary for managing customer success: listening.

Endnotes

[1] Cited in "Master the Art of Customer Loyalty" by V. Ho, March 14, 2013. Retrieved from http://www.inc.com/victor-ho/master-the-art-of-customer-loyalty.html.

[2] http://mblaisdell.com/2012/06/15/no-churn-customer-success-and-the-valuation-of-a-saas-company/.

[3] "Measuring the ROI of Customer Success Management Solutions," Gainsight-Mainstay, 2014, page 6, www.slideshare.net/MainstayCompany/gainsight-roi-for-csm-wp-9.

[4] Cited in "Customer Loyalty" by Jill Griffin. http://altfeldinc.com/pdfs/Customer%20Loyalty.pdf.

[5] "Measuring the ROI of Customer Success Management Solutions," Gainsight-Mainstay, 2014, page 6. http://www.slideshare.net/MainstayCompany/gainsight-roi-for-csm-wp-9.

[6] "What's a brand advocate worth?" Zuberance Whitepaper, 2010.

[7] IDC, 2009, as cited in "ROI Based Marketing and Sales Strategy" by Glenn Clowney. http://www.evancarmichael.com/library/glenn-clowney/ROI-Based-Marketing-and-Sales-Strategy.html.

[8] Tomasz Tunguz, "How Customer Success Meaningfully Reduces Cost of Customer Acquisition." http://tomtunguz.com/customer-success-cac/.

3 ————————————————————————

Listen

"It is the province of knowledge to speak and it is the privilege of wisdom to listen."

–Oliver Wendell Holmes

In this chapter we'll delve deeper into what it means to really *listen* to your customers and why it's such a critical part of engaging them strategically to assure success. We will argue that creating an effective listening capability is the very first step in the process of building an effective customer success strategy—one that will equip your business to thrive in the customer-first Subscription Economy. We believe that listening is the foundation for customer success. Yet surprisingly few businesses get listening right.

Your customer success strategy is only as good as your ability to know what it really means for your customer to be successful, and acquiring that understanding is entirely dependent on how well you listen to your customers. Only through *continuous, systematic, and disciplined listening* can you grasp every aspect of how your customers view their business, what kinds of business outcomes they are seeking, and—perhaps most crucially—how you can help them achieve those outcomes.

In our experience, the most successful customer listening programs include the following elements:

- **Selective and continuous input.** Effective listening is taking the pulse of your customers *continuously* by collecting a *targeted range of feedback,* including not just satisfaction assessments, but measures of how successfully (and broadly) your product is being adopted, and how it's adding value to their business.

- **Identification of key themes.** Listening platforms need to be able to efficiently sort and analyze feedback to identify common experiences, opinions, and themes expressed by multiple customers, across various customer segments.

- **Closed-loop response mechanisms.** Customer feedback must be managed in a way that enables you to take decisive action in a timely and effective fashion.

Gathering input from customers isn't a new concept. This chapter is more about how you can capture a new form of feedback and then concentrate your efforts on improving what you do to make your customer more successful. The basic measures of success are found in a combination of leading and trailing indicators of whether your customers are actually attaining the business outcomes they sought. Thus, what is measured is tightly connected to customer attainment of business outcomes operationally, financially, and strategically.

Fact: Only 55% of B2B enterprises say they understand how their customers measure success.
Source: Competing for Customers research, 2016

Setting Up "Listening Posts"

We use the term "listening posts" to describe the range of people, processes, and platforms (technologies) that companies deploy to gather feedback from customers. Listening posts encompass many different customer interactions points, including:

- Customer satisfaction, net promoter, loyalty, and success surveys
- Customer advisory boards and focus groups
- Sales transactions and other engagements
- Customer service interactions
- Marketing interactions
- Embedded hardware and software that track product usage and performance
- Tracking of website visits, downloads, and other indicators of customer digital and physical engagement
- Social media tracking
- Executive briefing and product roadmap commentary
- Quarterly business reviews

As you might imagine from looking at this list, listening posts can capture both *structured* feedback (quantitative information such as sales records, the number and types of service tickets logged, satisfaction ratings on a 1-10 scale, and so forth) and *unstructured* feedback (qualitative sentiment expressed in meetings, e-mails, social media, and other customer interactions). Although the techniques for capturing structured feedback are tried and true, increasingly companies are investing in new technologies, such as big data analytics, to uncover insights hidden in unstructured customer input and combine that with the structured input.

In the past few years, we've seen companies set up an increasing number and variety of listening posts, adding to traditional mechanisms like simple "tell us what you think" after-sale surveys. We are seeing substantial investments in new systems that pull in large volumes of data, creating a torrent of customer feedback that requires expert analysis and sophisticated tools to makes sense of. This explains why so many companies are rushing to hire data scientists and implementing advanced databases and analytic technologies. Such investments are absolutely essential to successfully compete in the new economy.

Know Thy Customer

To get the greatest benefit from listening, you need to tune in to the right people. Think of your customer as an actual person whose role will vary according to his or her job function, line of business, and place in the customer lifecycle. Key distinctions also include whether the individual is an end user, a business manager or executive, a technologist, a decision maker, or a key influencer of buying decisions. These distinctions are often overlapping, as is the case with a chief information officer, chief marketing officer, or chief human resources officer.

What can you learn from listening? For Oracle a concerted listening program helps it learn what matters most to its customers' top executives and what drives them to continue buying from the company. The company's listening efforts include a multi-pronged survey that, in part, asks customer executives to rank a range of product, services, and relationship factors that are then correlated with overall satisfaction and loyalty. As shown in Figure 3.1, product satisfaction, understanding of business issues, acting as a trusted advisor, providing relevant information, and realization of value are the five factors that have the biggest impact on the loyalty of these executives. The perception of this vendor as a "trusted advisor" shows marked improvement (20%) over a four-year period. By correlating this survey to revenue data, Oracle further found that customers that show positive movement in these five factors are not only more loyal, but also spend more over time. It's the ability of this company, and your company, to identify new ways to correlate and analyze data from a myriad of listening posts that will improve sales performance by helping you explore new opportunities to engage and ensure your customers' success.

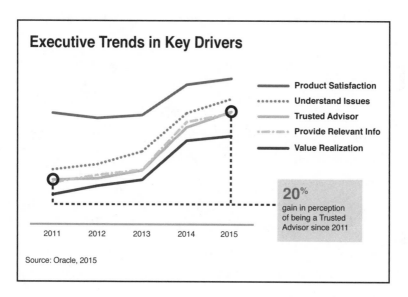

Figure 3.1 Listening tells you what matters most to your customers.

Collecting Structured Feedback: The Customer Survey

The most common vehicle for collecting *structured* feedback is the traditional survey, which allows you to organize and explore responses in an easily analyzed structure. There are many types of surveys and survey tools out there. Web-based surveys are by far the most popular, and there are a number of easy-to-use and powerful tools on the market. But the particular survey tools and methods you choose are less important than figuring out what information to collect, when to collect it, and from which customers (including specific groups and individuals within a given customer organization).

Surveys can be narrow or broad, and target specific individuals or wide swaths of your customer base. The information sought can range from the very tactical, such as the usefulness of individual product features, to the very strategic, such as realization of value and business outcomes.

It's in this last category—customer success—where we believe more companies can benefit through the use of well-designed surveys. Here we recommend gathering input at various "moments" or stages across the customer's lifecycles. We break down that lifecycle into four stages, as described below and illustrated in Figure 3.2:

- **Define.** When the customer is examining its strategic, operational, and/or financial needs and clarifying the business outcomes it wants to achieve.

- **Buy.** When the customer is actively comparing vendors, requesting proposals, and negotiating deals.

- **Use.** When the customer has purchased the solution and is in the process of deploying and actually using the products and services.

- **Succeed.** When the customer is realizing business outcomes and benefits from the products or services.

Source: Competing for Customers, 2016

Figure 3.2 The customer lifecycle.

The best listening programs should define how each lifecycle phase affects customer success, and then capture feedback that helps you gauge how well you are enabling that success. We've proposed a series of seven steps that are mapped to the lifecycle phases. These steps (and associated questions) are designed to help you define the right survey attributes that will ultimately confirm whether you are engaging your customer in a way that yields positive business outcomes. Figure 3.3 details the process.

Lifecycle	Process Steps and Questions
Define	**Step 1: Define the Customer's Need** – Do you understand your customer's business and how they are measured relative to their competitors? Do you assist with strategic planning, with an understanding of business issues and priorities?
	Step 2: Research Solution Options with Your Customer – Do you present your capabilities in the language your customer uses for defining the need and identifying candidate products or solutions? Do you provide objective guidance in identifying the best solution?
	Step 3: Support the Customer's Selection Process – Do you present a business case to your customer, helping to justify the investment? Is the quoting process straightforward, with clear pricing?
Buy	**Step 4: Create a Frictionless Buying Process** – Do you provide an ordering process that is straightforward, transparent, and presents the customer with an easy and frictionless experience? Is your customer able to buy from you in a consistent manner, across all products and services?
Use	**Step 5: Support the Solution Adoption** – Do you help your customer implement your solution and then guide them on an ongoing basis on continuously improving solution adoption?
Succeed	**Step 6: Maintain the Value of Your Solution** – Do you solicit ongoing feedback from your customer on if and how you are enabling them to realize value and achieve desired business outcomes? Do you give your customer guidance on usage best practices? Is their support experience consistent across products?
	Step 7: Enable Customers to Recommend Your Solution – Does your customer actively advocate for you, and do they do so in terms that demonstrate how you directly contribute to the customer achieving desired business outcomes?

Source: Competing for Customers, 2016

Figure 3.3 Listening for the right information at critical moments in the customer lifecycle.

You can dramatically increase the effectiveness of your listening posts by adopting two best practices: First, be sure to time your data collection to match key customer milestones in the lifecycle; and second, ask questions that explore your customer's unique business and the unique ways you engage with that customer. Beyond alerting you to emerging problems you can take action on, this approach can also let you know when a customer could be ready to buy more or be an advocate for you.

Unstructured Feedback: The Power of Storytelling

Structured surveys are a necessary part of any good listening program, but they won't give you a complete—or even accurate—picture of what your customers are thinking. Not everyone wants to fill out a survey, so you may be missing input from key people. And surveys are ineffective at capturing the kind of nuanced opinions that are embedded in the open-ended conversations that your customers have every day. Consequently, the best listening programs incorporate qualitative (unstructured) feedback from sources such as these:

- One-to-one customer interactions
- Customer advisory boards
- Focus groups
- Input from your employees who directly serve customers
- Social media
- Product development road map sessions
- Quarterly business reviews

The benefits of collecting qualitative input are twofold. First, anecdotes will effectively corroborate (or challenge) your survey results; second, you get invaluable stories about your customers, told in their own words. The feedback you get from candid, live interactions with customers (and between them) is often the best way to determine whether your customers are achieving their desired business outcomes and whether you are doing enough to support that effort.

Aligning Customers and Employees: Both Sides of the Same Story

When you're listening to your customers, don't forget to take the pulse of your own employees as well. If your employees are expressing sentiments that are completely at odds with what your customers are saying, then you'll likely face an uphill battle in delivering success for your customers. The most highly customer-focused organizations we know are the ones that have made it a point of aligning employee input with customer input—and they do that by synchronizing and reconciling employee and customer feedback.

Oracle's CEO Mark Hurd, for example, conducts a periodic survey of employees to solicit their views across an array of topics, including their efficiency and effectiveness in working with customers. The surveys have found that workers sometimes struggle with the complexity and timeliness of basic business tasks such as quoting, ordering, and contract execution. What do customers think? Surveys and other feedback have revealed similar frustrations, with certain customers declaring that this aspect of the relationship with Oracle could be an impediment to success.

With both sides of the fence in agreement, Oracle has invested heavily in initiatives to streamline contracting and other customer-facing processes to reduce friction between buyer and seller. This is making it easier for customers to do business with Oracle and is driving internal efficiencies at the same time.

Instrumenting for Success: Boosting Your Listening Power

The Internet of Things (IoT) is changing everything. It is transforming medicine with sensor-enabled pill bottles, remote EKG devices, and myriad other forms of instrumentation, including wearable and ingestible diagnostics. In most every industry, instrumentation is now making it possible to listen to the workings of your products and services everywhere they are used. Much hyped and mostly misunderstood, the IoT has at its core the idea of placing sensors—hardware and software—inside your products, making them "smart" and capable of communicating with other machines—and with you—over the Internet.

Internet-connected instrumentation is now opening up all kinds of possibilities for industry—from smart refrigerators to wind farms that talk to each other—creating a market estimated to be worth some $19 trillion by 2020.[1] It's also radically changing the way businesses listen to customers.

Rockwell Automation, for example, now embeds sensors and software into its machine controllers, allowing the company to "listen" to equipment installed at its customers' factories. GE similarly instruments its jet engines to monitor themselves for signs of trouble during flights. The engines provide a continuous data feed to ground crews, preparing them for maintenance tasks even before the plane lands. The company's power subsidiary connects its gas turbines to the cloud, tapping into software and analytics that enable power plants to maximize heat output with the greatest possible efficiency. Oracle instruments its engineered systems with "phone home" capabilities so performance is continuously monitored. As a result, Oracle often identifies and fixes a problem before the customer is even aware.

In effect, the Internet of Things can turn your *products* into listening posts, feeding you data on everything from how the product is being used to signs of an impending malfunction. Unlike Web surveys, instrumented products can send you feedback *continuously*, telling you if and how your customers are using your products—in a non-invasive way that can yield *leading* instead of *trailing* indicators. Either way, you now have the data you need to take effective action to deliver the outcomes your customer wants.

What's more, you can correlate smart-machine feedback with conventionally gathered feedback (via surveys, for example) to help you identify "moments of truth"—those events or interactions that have the greatest impact on customer experience. Add operational, financial, and other data to the mix and you get a truly holistic view of what drives your customers' behavior. Further refine the intelligence collected with modern analytic tools, including big data, and you can see patterns never before visible.

A great example of "moments of truth" in action was employed by Cisco, the global networking company. Listening to its energy customers, Cisco created an industry solution called a "rig in a box." This solution was conceived through a variety of listening posts including executive briefings, co-product development sessions, and pilot data gathering. The impact of the solution is truly transformational for energy-producing companies. The ability now to proactively monitor and manage rigs that are often located in desolate and dangerous areas of the world has greatly reduced costs, increased production and revenue, reduced risks, and increased operational accuracy.

Further, as we'll discuss in Chapter 8, "How GE Power Fuels Growth by Delivering Outcomes," the spread of the Internet of Things will spur the deployment of a new generation of self-learning, self-maintaining, and self-optimizing products, which will help companies ensure concrete operational and business outcomes. Indeed, this is already becoming a reality at many of the companies we've studied.

The Internet of What?

How did they come up with the name for one of our favorite new technology buzz phrases, the Internet of Things? "It all started with lipstick," say authors Kevin and Alison Maney. Specifically, it was a "particularly popular color of Oil of Olay lipstick that Kevin Ashton had been pushing as a brand manager at Procter & Gamble and it was perpetually out of stock. He decided to find out why, and found holes in data about the supply chain that eventually led him to drive the early deployment of RFID (radio frequency identification) chips on inventory. Asked by the Massachusetts Institute of Technology to start a group that would research RFID technology, he found a way to talk about RFID to a less-than-computer-savvy crowd—by coining the phrase the Internet of Things or IoT."

From Kevin Ashton, Father of the Internet of Things and Network Trailblazer[2]

Measures of Success

Every customer measures success differently, which is precisely why listening is such an essential skill to master if you want to make sure your customers in fact succeed. But to maximize the value of listening—that is, to elicit the responses that reveal the outcomes important to your customers—you need to ask the right questions.

Here is a list of questions to get you started. Naturally, the questions you ask will need to be tailored to your customer's specific business, and will also depend on where they are in the customer lifecycle.

- How do you measure success—at individual, departmental, line of business, and leadership levels?
- How are our products and services contributing to that success?

- When our products aren't fully adopted and operating at their full potential, what is the impact on your success?
- What is inhibiting adoption of our products/services, and what recommendations would you make to achieve full potential?
- What would improvements in adopting our products/services mean in terms of improvements to your success measures?
- What competitive or disruptive technologies, products, or services are threatening adoption and how might we help you address them?

Closing the Loop

If you're asking all the right questions about how your products and services impact your customers' success, you're already ahead of the game. Your next step is to organize the raw data coming in through your listening posts, make sense of it, and take appropriate actions in response. Figure 3.4 shows a basic process flow.

Collect Anecdotes and Develop Hypotheses

Taking the pulse of your customers is the first critical step in listening. By that we mean collecting informal or anecdotal evidence of your customer's concerns, challenges, or opportunities. Use these "soft" data points to create a set of questions, or hypotheses, that provide the foundation for further investigation. The objective is to assess whether these initial, informal impressions truly point to better ways to engage with your customers and drive customer success.

Forming hypotheses about what this unstructured data is telling you gives you a framework for structured data collection, analysis, and storytelling. Hypotheses should also be informed by your own hunches about problem areas that need attention: ineffective account management, product quality issues, cumbersome commercial processes, poor sales tactics, and the like.

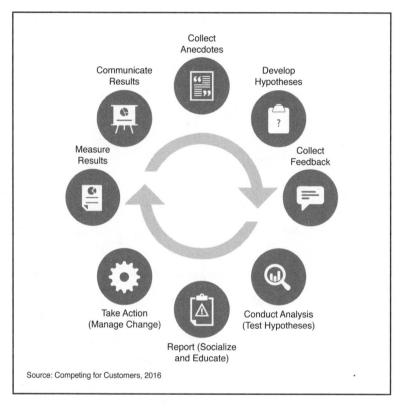

Figure 3.4 Closing the feedback loop.

Collect Feedback and Conduct Analysis

Once you have a set of hypotheses, it's time to prove or disprove them by collecting structured feedback from the surveys and other operational and transactional sources we discussed previously. Fortunately, new tools are available that can help streamline this chore, many of them leveraging big data and other advanced business analytics applications to spot patterns in a mass of qualitative and quantitative data. Such tools automate much of the drill-downs and what-if scenarios so that you spend less time packaging the feedback and more time exploring the data and getting to findings and actions. Ultimately, the objective of these analytics is to give you a unified view of the customer and empower you to take action based on the story the feedback tells you.

Report and Take Action

We recommend making your ongoing analysis—as well as the underlying data—available continuously to a hand-picked group of executives and managers across the organization. Supplement that with a broader reporting process, in which point-in-time snapshots are presented to lower levels of the organization for review, action, and communication.

We suggest delivering the results to upper management in a comprehensive "voice of the customer" communication, starting with the most senior executives and even the board of directors. We also recommend creating a set of role-based presentations enabling review of the data across business units. The most advanced organizations, including Oracle, use these presentations to facilitate executive workshops, ensuring consistent and accurate interpretation of data, as well as aggressive implementation of changes to address the feedback. Oracle, for one, delivers more than 100 of these workshops across the company every six months.

Creating the most compelling customer stories through the use of listening posts, presented to the right people in your organization, is key, but not sufficient. You also have to empower the organization with analytical and change-management tools to promote acceptance, refinement, and action. We will discuss strategies for taking action in

Chapter 7, "Ensure." The ability to prioritize actions based on careful listening is critical given the limited resources, attention, and time most organizations have available to carry out these actions.

Measure and Communicate Results

Lastly, once your action plans are underway, it's time to implement a measurement system that continuously assesses progress. From the organizations we have examined, we are typically seeing a positive shift of customer sentiment roughly 12-18 months after corrective actions have been taken. Once this shift becomes evident, that's the time to communicate back to your customers, describing your objectives, progress, and results. We've found that simply compelling your customers to provide you with detailed feedback without also demonstrating what you did with that feedback is invariably disastrous.

Getting Started

Laying the foundation for listening to your customers requires you to take a hard look at where you are today and then build on the elements you have that are most effective. Start by assessing your current position against a simple maturity model to give you a clear view of your desired end state and what your objectives should be.

Many organizations today have customer centricity programs in place with tools and processes for determining satisfaction and loyalty measures. The more advanced programs have additional customer feedback and collaboration mechanisms for addressing the fundamentals of creating value for customers. The most forward-thinking programs continually assess whether customers' business needs are being met, and they do so through a system of listening posts.

Our goal here is not to discourage you. We want you to have a view of what the possibilities are, what your current standing is, and next steps you can take to move forward with a world-class listening capability.

In the next chapter you will learn about an innovative company called Telogis and the advances it has made in listening to customers. After that, we dive into the second major driver of customer success: engagement.

Endnotes

[1] "Cisco CEO Pegs Internet of Things as $19 Trillion Market," Bloomberg, 1/7/2014.

[2] "Kevin Ashton: Trailblazer & Father of the Internet of Things," Cisco, Kevin Maney, 12/8/2014.

4

Telogis Listens for Success

"Because the subscription economy drives a business outcome focus, all of the things we know about customer loyalty and experience are even more accentuated and we must be more attuned to it than 10 to 15 years ago."

—David Cozzens, CEO of Telogis

Telogis leads a pack of new companies that are reinventing the way businesses move materials, services, and products from point A to point B. By harnessing breakthrough technologies such as the Internet of Things, big data, and cloud computing, Telogis is revolutionizing how companies manage mobile assets—everything from truck fleets to heavy equipment—and the workforces that operate them.

Imagine a construction firm tracking—to the hour—how much asphalt its trucks have poured and how long each driver has been on the road. That's now a reality thanks to Telogis's cloud-based connected technologies, which are helping companies maximize asset value, streamline supply chains, and comply with a tangle of industry regulations. Soft drink bottling and distribution king Coca Cola Refreshments relies on Telogis to shave fuel bills and deliver bottled beverages to more than a million destinations across the U.S. each day.

Telogis's technology has become so popular with shippers that major vehicle makers such as Ford, GM, and Volvo Trucks have started installing Telogis software into new trucks and customers just switch it on. The spread of Telogis's platform worldwide has fueled a long run of double-digit growth: In 2014, industry consultant Deloitte ranked Telogis as one of North America's fastest-growing technology companies for the seventh year in a row.

How can you explain Telogis's outsized success at competing for customers? We believe one of the keys has been a corporate culture built around the goal of customer success. In this chapter we'll focus on the company's unique qualities that helped it capture a big lead in the race for customers—most notably its conscious habit of listening closely to customers before, during, and after the sale.

CEO Dave Cozzens has been instrumental in instilling this uniquely customer-centric culture at Telogis. Arriving at Telogis in 2007 after stints at a handful of top technology enterprises, including software maker Novell, Cozzens saw firsthand the rapid market shifts that took place in the networking industry of the 1990s. Exposure to that era prepared him for today's even bigger shift to the subscription-based economy.

He also had a chance to study the different ways companies stand out in the market and create competitive advantage. His conclusion: The more you understand your customer's business—including what makes *their* customers tick—the more successful you'll be at building long-term relationships that pay off in recurring, ever-expanding sales. This idea formed the heart of the customer-first culture he brought to Telogis.

Listening First

One of the interesting features of this culture is that Telogis deliberately avoids the hard sell, preferring to start every customer relationship with a clean slate. Unless requested by the prospective customer, specific products are seldom discussed at the first meeting. Instead, Telogis likes to delve deeply into how the prospect's business works, where it wants to go, and the major challenges it faces. Invariably, much time is spent discussing and validating different strategies and options. Opportunities for cost savings are explored, and not infrequently the talk turns to "business transformation" and how Telogis can help the customer enable new revenue models. Only later will sales teams explain how Telogis products and services can solve for these challenges and open up strategic opportunities.

The decision to put direct sales pitches on the back burner wasn't an easy one. After all, it would mean incurring higher selling costs early in the relationship. But executives were betting that companies would spend more over the long run if they saw Telogis not as an equipment vendor but as a strategic partner—a true business advisor to help invent better ways to serve their customers.

All of this marks a big departure from the traditional approach of chalking up sales early and often—of closing deals and walking away. To make this new model work, Telogis needed to commit to longer-term customer relationships and place a significantly higher value on retention. New consultative and relationship-building skills would need to be developed in the organization.

Telogis: Key Takeaways

Here are some customer success strategies that logistics innovator Telogis uses to stay head of the competition:

- Invest in your customers early and develop a strategic view of your value to the customer.

- Create a culture of customer success across the entire company.

- Organize and incentivize your sales and marketing teams to promote retention and expansion—not just acquisition.

- Ensure that your marketing programs provide clear evidence of the business value you're delivering beyond the initial sale.

- The practice of customer success delivery is still in its infancy, so remain active and participate in defining the field.

Avoiding Bottlenecks

Coca-Cola Refreshments, whose drivers visit more than a million drop-off points a day, uses Telogis technology to spot delivery "bottlenecks" in real time and continuously optimize route designs.

Thriving in the Subscription Economy

Telogis believes that as customers spend more time using its platform, more opportunities will arise to serve them. That is why it places a high priority on continuously learning about the state of the customer's business and using these insights to direct customers toward new services that could generate additional business value.

Timing—and patience—is often critical. For example, a customer may need to wait until it realizes savings from optimized vehicle routing before it can afford to add other advanced capabilities. Steady listening, learning, and relationship building are key to seizing these emerging opportunities for enabling customer success.

Telogis holds quarterly business reviews to stay in sync with customers. The sessions cover the status of current deployments and also provide a chance to brainstorm ways to expand the reach of these systems. More often than not, the reviews open the customer's eyes to unexpected opportunities. For example, a company initially interested in only tracking truck movements may learn that it can also empower its workforce by adding a gamelike tool that incentivizes drivers to boost safety and operational efficiency.

Actually, the idea for this tool was born during one of Telogis's customer-listening sessions. "They asked us a simple question," Cozzens says. "Is there a way to tell the driver to slow down when they are going too fast?" Before long, Telogis had introduced its popular Telogis Coach application, a real-time "scorecard" that shows drivers how well they're complying with speed, other driver behavior guidelines, and meeting customer satisfaction goals.

The tool's "leaderboard"—viewable by an entire team of drivers—creates a competitive atmosphere that spurs better driving and ultimately better business results. The application also enables companies to design employee rewards and incentive programs so that individual drivers can be recognized and potentially compensated for outstanding performance.

Delivering Value from Day One

Telogis quickly figured out that surviving and thriving in the Subscription Economy would be much different than in the old "pack and ship" software days when a customer's bad decision could not be so easily undone. In today's software-as-a-service (SaaS) world, unhappy customers need only cancel their subscription. That's why Telogis can never assume that each sale is permanent. The company needs to deliver value from day one—and beyond—or risk losing that customer.

With subscriber attrition always looming, Telogis has mobilized teams of customer advocates—called "customer success principals"—specifically tasked with boosting retention. The teams get involved right after a sale, helping oversee the implementation and smoothing out early bumps in the road. The group also works to estimate specific business outcomes companies can expect when the mobile-asset platform is fully deployed. Later, the team measures actual results and helps customers fine-tune the application to squeeze out more efficiency. Throughout the process, Telogis's highly specialized resources continue to probe for additional business transformation opportunities.

Signs of Success

How can you tell that customers love Telogis? Almost without exception, the internal customer sponsors who recommended Telogis have been subsequently rewarded with promotions. As CEO Cozzens points out: "We can't take credit for getting them promoted, but we definitely didn't get them fired!"

Blurring the Lines

To get ahead in the subscription economy, Telogis's CEO says that traditional organizational structures need to be radically revised. "To be successful, you need to blur the lines between professional services, account management, and technical support," he says. "Everyone needs to be focused on customer success."

To rally teams around this single purpose, Telogis reformulated its job definitions and restructured its monetary incentives. It now ties sales compensation to recurring revenues and retention—not just initial sales—and rewards both sales reps and customer success principals in a way that stresses the importance of both roles in achieving success.

Executives say that aligning the organization correctly is necessary to generate the retention levels and revenue momentum required to pay for early-cycle sales costs. "The customer success approach would collapse under its own weight," Cozzens explains. "It's really part of the economics of the SaaS business model that if you can't figure out how to retain and up-sell customers, the economics just don't work."

Pushing Forward

Telogis's shift in emphasis from acquiring customers to retaining them called for a fresh approach to marketing, including devoting more resources to post-sale education and awareness building. More than ever, you'll see Telogis reminding customers of the extra business value they can realize by activating new features and services. "We are always pushing the customer forward," Cozzens says, adding that post-sale marketing programs are critical to sustaining demand. Telogis also pays special attention to its network of resellers that serves small and medium-sized customers. The company primes this channel with a range of marketing campaigns focused on retention and up-selling.

It's no surprise to hear that customers—rather than products—take center stage at the company's annual Telogis Latitude conference. Indeed, the first day of the conference is devoted entirely to customer presentations and success stories—providing yet another great listening opportunity, by the way. It's not until the second day that Telogis turns the spotlight on its products.

Tackling the Future

Telogis hones its listening skills by participating in industry groups such as the Technology Services Industry Association, whose customer success and leadership forum is a great place to trade customer success strategies and best practices with industry leaders. Telogis also gathers customer success intelligence through research sponsored by the association.

Listening to customers will always remain a core tenet of Telogis's business model as it tackles new markets and services. And an open-minded attitude will go hand-in-hand with this strategy, Cozzens says: "We don't have this all figured out yet and keep asking ourselves, 'What's everyone else doing?'" For Telogis, listening carefully to the answers to these questions will undoubtedly underpin its strategy for conquering the next big technology transition.

5

Engage

"It is so much easier to be nice, to be respectful, to put your-self in your customers' shoes and try to understand how you might help them before they ask for help, than it is to try to mend a broken customer relationship."

–Mark Cuban

As we discussed in Chapter 3, "Listen," setting up listening posts to capture, analyze, and act on customer feedback helps create a strong foundation for ensuring customer success. In this chapter we focus on how you can leverage the insights and opportunities gleaned from careful listening to engage with customers in creative new ways and deliver better business outcomes. Our belief is that to succeed in the Subscription Economy—and fulfill next-generation customer expectations—you will need to fundamentally transform your existing sales, marketing, professional services, support, and product development processes. The new model of strategic customer engagement is designed to deliver business outcomes by enabling you to do the following:

- **Become a valued, strategic partner to your customers.** Strategic customer engagements position you to be an invaluable resource to your customers by building a highly collaborative relationship—one that ultimately influences the strategic direction of *both you and your customer.*

- **Become a thought leader in your market.** Engaging with your customers in new ways allows you to capitalize on the expertise you've gained in critical market segments and industries to educate your customers on the latest developments in technology, markets, and regulations, including how and when they may impact their business.

- **Provide comprehensive, successful solutions.** When you engage your customers strategically, you use a range of consultative skills to help you make the case to top executives, customize your product or solution to fit the customer's unique needs, ensure a successful implementation, and identify new solutions that could add value down the road.

So does strategic customer engagement work? Our research, detailed in this chapter, shows that it does pay off—indeed, handsomely, if done right—by redefining your customer experiences to differentiate you from your competition.

In a recent paper for the *Harvard Business Review*,[1] Peter Kriss, a senior research scientist for Medallian, examined the performance of companies that employed strategic engagement techniques to improve the customer experience. The result: Customers with the best experiences spent 140% more than those with the poorest experiences, as shown in Figure 5.1. Those with great experiences also tended to stay around longer, with annual retention rates nearly twice as high as the lower category, and a total customer "life span" that lasted six years longer on average, as shown in Figure 5.2. Strategic engagements can also lower service costs, Kriss discovered. Telecom giant Sprint, for example, found that by boosting customer experience, it could reduce customer service costs by as much as a third.

Figure 5.1 Customer experience drives sales.

Figure 5.2 Customer experience drives membership.

Telogis is another example. This leader in cloud-based transportation intelligence, profiled in Chapter 4, "Telogis Listens for Success," created a strategic customer engagement program unlike that of any of its competitors. The program supercharged sales almost immediately. In fact, Telogis executives cite it as a major factor contributing to the company's six years of growth and continuing market leadership.

Creating a truly strategic customer engagement capability necessarily involves the entire business. That's why the existence of "silos" separating different business functions frequently gets in the way of effective customer engagements. So can frequent turf battles, poorly designed management incentives, and simply an unwillingness of executives to address outmoded, ineffective business practices. For example, sales teams that are too rigidly focused on closing deals can be an impediment to effective engagements, trading short-term revenue for the long-term growth and profitability of the customer relationship.

When groups work in isolation, disconnects frequently crop up that can derail strategic customer engagements. Sales and marketing, for example, are famous for not talking to each other. This may explain why many marketing teams, lacking feedback from frontline sales reps, keep producing fluffy brochures that provide no value whatsoever in the customer's decision-making process. These situations are further complicated when you have multiple sales reps or teams calling on the same customer, unless there is a systematic way to connect them and open the lines of communication.

Organizational walls may also explain why product developers regularly miss the mark with customers. We saw this firsthand with a multibillion-dollar telecom provider that was trying to sell phone services to universities. The technology behind the service was superb, but unfortunately product developers had insisted on a convoluted licensing arrangement that required customers to keep an updated list of the names of every user. University CIOs were flummoxed by the requirement, especially considering that 25% to 30% of all the "users"—namely, students—graduate each year. Not surprisingly, deals were dead on arrival. Had the telecom been more strategically engaged with and attuned to its customers, developers would have never brought this product to market in this manner.

Service and support teams also need to figure prominently in the strategic engagement process. In the new customer-first Subscription Economy, customers no longer tolerate service delays and waste no time looking at other vendors that can provide proactive support. It's no coincidence that leaders in strategic engagement are investing heavily in big data and IoT-enabled technologies to predict and fix customer service issues without the customer knowing about it.

To create a strategic customer engagement capability, companies need to work more holistically. That often means tearing down "functional silos," bringing in talent with fresh perspectives, and investing in systems, processes, and tools that help you engage customers in strategic new ways.

The winners in the Subscription Economy will be companies that deliver on their promises of business impact. Achieving that will hinge on their ability to engage effectively with customers and drive that impact incrementally.

We'll now explore how leaders in strategic customer engagement are addressing these questions and setting themselves up for success in the Subscription Economy. We've divided the discussion by functional areas, such as sales, marketing, and service, since many companies will need to reinvent the way they do business in multiple areas. For each area, we provide guidance for how to transform teams into strategic customer engagement organizations.

Marketing: Storytelling with a Business Impact

Like every other aspect of your business, marketing will need to adapt to the realities of the new economy. Not that marketing's usual job of spreading brand awareness and generating leads will go away. Those tasks will always be necessary. But marketing will need to infuse everything they do with a new vision built for the customer-first revolution and Subscription Economy.

Thriving in the new era will require your marketing to become more "strategic." By that we mean that you'll need to show customers not just that your products work as advertised, but, more importantly, that they deliver the business outcomes your customers need in order to stay ahead in a fundamentally altered market landscape. To put it another way, you will need to become a thought leader in your industry. Great marketing will position your company as a strategic partner that understands the underlying drivers of value in your customers' business today, and what is likely to drive it ten years from now. Longer-term assurances are critical in an economy in which fewer customers are saddled with huge up-front capital outlays, and switching costs are shrinking.

Can you share a vision of how your customer will grow and prosper with your company, and continue to reap value beyond the initial sale? How will you help your customers navigate difficult transition periods? Will you be there for them when the going gets tough? The stories you tell your customers will need to be grounded in measures of business impact, and based on credible, provable demonstrations of value.

The End of Fluff

Nothing is more annoying to modern business buyers than marketing fluff. A lot of it is due to the "fill the bucket" mentality among old-line marketers, which values quantity over quality. Digitization has changed the landscape, as has the shift to outcomes-oriented buying patterns. Fluff is out. Quantified evidence of business impact is in. Overflowing buckets of hype have been replaced by digital multimedia, customer segmentation, personalized messaging, and a clear view of the customer engagement model spanning the entire customer experience.

Fluff marketing likely won't go away entirely, but increasingly it lacks the pull-through of true evidence-based marketing that turns on business value, revenue generation, and the quantified successes of similar customers. Assembling the evidence will require you to make the effort to engage with your customers to detail how they're benefiting from your products. Those interactions can also pry open the door to additional sales and marketing opportunities.

You might start with a whitepaper that positions your company as a thought leader in your industry—or as an innovator and a disruptor (in the good sense of the word). Then use that research to economically create videos, case studies, and infographics to further solidify your position. At the core of this strategy are researched customer proof points that very specifically talk to the engagement model those customers experienced and the value they realized. We call this approach "research once, leverage often," and it's one of the most effective ways to get the most out of your marketing dollars (see Figure 5.3).

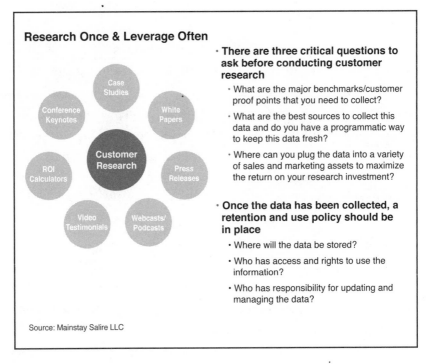

Research Once & Leverage Often

- **There are three critical questions to ask before conducting customer research**
  - What are the major benchmarks/customer proof points that you need to collect?
  - What are the best sources to collect this data and do you have a programmatic way to keep this data fresh?
  - Where can you plug the data into a variety of sales and marketing assets to maximize the return on your research investment?

- **Once the data has been collected, a retention and use policy should be in place**
  - Where will the data be stored?
  - Who has access and rights to use the information?
  - Who has responsibility for updating and managing the data?

Source: Mainstay Salire LLC

Figure 5.3 Research once, leverage often.

Lifecycle Marketing

Modern marketers must take a leadership role in delivering the right information to customers at the right time. This goes far beyond traditional awareness building and lead generation. Each stage of the customer lifecycle calls for different types of marketing activities and content, and will utilize different operational groups across your company. Marketing's job becomes coordinating those activities and content in a way that answers the basic question your customers will have. For example, when your customers are in the early stages of exploring solutions to a specific challenge, you need to help those customers understand how your products and solutions can help them compete more effectively. You will also need to provide compelling evidence that you are an effective business partner and trusted advisor.

Figure 5.4 provides a series of questions that your customers should be contemplating. The job of marketing is to orchestrate the answers that will demonstrate your focus on customer success by delivering business outcomes.

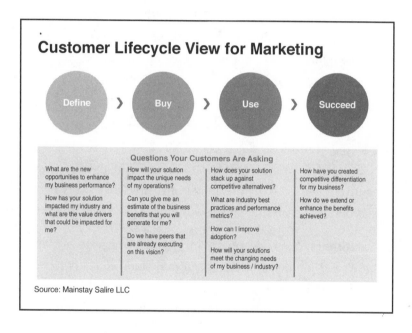

Figure 5.4 Marketing for customer success.

Often we find that marketing organizations can answer only a few of these questions—generally in the earlier stages—lacking the perspective, right relationships, and customer touch points to properly cover the full lifecycle. As a result, we've seen many companies fall into "content traps"—where the marketing efforts and materials completely miss what customers are looking for—such as vague messaging, pie in the sky promises, no depth (soft benefits), and lack of follow through. These traps can be avoided entirely by starting with value realized and then working backward to the customer actions that deliver the value and the engagement that drives those actions. These elements, of course, vary as a function of where you are in the lifecycle.

Getting Personal

Marketing works best when it speaks to you personally—when the company knows who you are and what you need in order to be successful at your job. That's why modern marketers increasingly focus on individualizing the messages they create and targeting specific types of people—or personas—in their campaigns.

Remember too that you need to equip and enable *all* the different people in your organization who interact with those personas, so it helps to put yourself in the shoes of all these "constituents" who strategically engage your customers—from reselling partners to your top executives. Let's discuss the range of people marketers need to address as part of a customer success-oriented marketing program:

- **Customers.** Your customers include a menagerie of personalities and job descriptions, from rank-and-file users to senior executives. So developing a persona-based marketing approach is essential to maximizing the opportunity to create and sustain value. Do you know who actually makes the purchasing decision for your products? Often it's not the same person as the all-important "influencer" behind the decision. What's more, you must also be able to convince everyday users and technologists that your products will improve their lives.

- **Outside Partners.** Resellers, distributors, and other channel partners are pressed for time, often dividing their attention between numerous tasks and vendors. They can also be very narrowly focused. Your messaging needs to be easily consumable and tailored to their business and their audiences.

- **Field Sales Reps.** Mobile enablement is a must-have for the modern on-the-go sales rep who needs to call up presentations and videos on the fly from any device. Marketing needs to make it easy for reps to find and share the right content in any sales situation, and minimize time spent in the office creating content. It also needs to position the sales rep, to a degree, as a trusted advisor.

- **Inside Sales Reps.** These lead qualifiers and nurturers need messaging and scripts that are consistent with your other channels. Remember that they're likely to be talking to prospects who have already scoured your website and social channels, so avoiding mixed messages is key.

- **Sales Consultants.** These specialists field the toughest questions from your customer's most demanding stakeholders, so you need to supply them with powerful value assessment and ROI tools, executive presentations, and whitepapers to deliver the punch to close the biggest deal.

- **Customer Success Managers.** With their focus on lifetime value, customer success managers need to be able to relate marketing content to the daily adoption and use of the product so they can highlight the value created for your customers. This content simply doesn't exist today in most cases.

- **Renewal Reps.** These salespeople need to be in lock-step with your Customer Success Managers, helping the customer to see, on an ongoing basis, the value created versus the value promised to make the case for subscription renewal.

- **Executives.** More than anybody, your top executives embody your brand, so it's important they have an intuitive grasp of your company's mission and vision. They need compelling presentations, talking points, and—especially—customer anecdotes that can win over Wall Street and conference goers alike.

Harnessing Social Media

More than ever, your brand is being defined by people you have no control over. Social media and its legions of bloggers and online commenters have become powerful shapers of opinion in our culture and increasingly key influencers of corporate buyers and decision makers. Marketers can no longer afford to ignore digital channels such as Facebook, LinkedIn, Twitter, YouTube, TrustRadius, and IT Central Station, which if harnessed effectively, can enable you to marshal an army of advocates for your brand at relatively little cost.

As these channels continue to gain your buyer's attention, it's important to take a programmatic approach to managing advocacy content. Digital channels require a weekly cadence of pushing new content out to your audience or risk losing viewership. Many companies we work with are adding a "social media editor" to their ranks to manage content and monitor traffic. Others are using big data technologies to sift through comments and analyze trends in real time, and leveraging new tools to automate social media publishing and track what's popular.

Sales: Strategic Selling in the Subscription Economy

The seismic shifts rolling through the economy hit sales organizations especially hard. The Subscription Economy, which drastically reduces switching costs, will require sales teams to take a longer view and focus on maximizing the customer's *lifetime value*. However, that doesn't mean short-term sales quotas will ever go away. Customer retention will now play an equal if not dominant role in determining a company's success.

With a larger portion of revenue hinging on renewals, sales organizations will be asked to communicate how they can deliver value to customers on an ongoing basis, over the long run. The bottom line: To be successful in the new economy, companies will need to rethink the sales models and selling tactics they've used for years.

Sales teams compete in a dog-eat-dog world. Under pressure from capital markets to hit revenue targets every quarter, CEOs demand immediate results. And many buyers have grown accustomed to the pitbull salesperson who won't let go of an opportunity. We'd even argue that these "hunters" play an important role to help overcome bureaucratic procurement processes and the inertia common in large-scale organizations.

However, as the subscription model continues to spread and Wall Street catches on to the new value equation, we're seeing more businesses begin to change the way they manage sales opportunities. They are doing this in stages, often starting by *overlaying* their account teams with a new breed of salesperson specifically trained and focused on forging long-term strategic customer relationships and orchestrating the rest of the sales team. The secret is balancing short-term sales targets with the long-term needs of the customer.

Many companies today have taken steps in the direction of long-term strategic selling, but most are still working to build the capability. Remember the following as you start your journey:

- **Building strategic relationships takes time.** If you are currently calling on midlevel managers, it can take a year or two—with the right messaging and outreach plan—to build relationships at the executive level.

- **Thought leadership messaging is critical.** If you cannot convince your customer that your solution provides significant value to their business, you will never gain access to the senior business leaders. Having expert consultative resources to develop this messaging is critical.

- **Messengers are as important as the message.** You can have a compelling message, but without the right messenger it will be challenging to form long-standing strategic relationships. The skillset for these sales consultants, architects, and industry experts is part art, part science, and can be very much underappreciated by businesses.

Rules of Engagement

There are four basic "rules of engagement" you should follow to build a strategic selling capability:[2]

- **Rule #1: Build Customer Relationships Based on Trust.** Long-term industry leadership can be built only on enduring and trusting customer relationships. Deploying a sales "overlay team" focused on the customer's long-term success, overall relationship management, and sales team orchestration can help energize the trust-building process. These team members must have strong relationship management skills and be comfortable asking the tough questions that help push the customer in new directions.

Adding Pep to Sales

A few years ago, IBM enlisted several hundred executives in an effort called the Partnership Executive Program to build lasting relationships with customers. These "PEP executives" were not meant to replace account teams but rather to add continuity to the relationship by staying with their assigned accounts year after year, even if an executive moved on to a new role at IBM. PEP executives had no responsibility for day-to-day sales quotas, so they were in a great position to provide objective advice to customers, further reinforcing trust. IBM's key achievement: showing the customer that you *value the relationship over the transaction.*

- **Rule #2: Create a Business Case and Value Realization Program.** Strategic engagements are founded on demonstrating your commitment to delivering business outcomes. To do this, you'll need to develop expertise and create tools for measuring business value that are tailored to the customer's industry. Ideally you'll formalize these tools into a program in which you track and measure key performance indicators from before the sale to well after. We call the process "target, track, and measure," and the output can include value-based customer scorecards and business cases to help customers understand the full value they're realizing—and where improvements can be made.

- **Rule #3: Take an Outside-In View of Your Company.** No one likes bad news, but sooner or later every customer relationship goes through a rough patch. An effective way to deal with the inevitable bumps in the road is to own the bad news along with the good. By embracing criticism, you can capture candid customer feedback that can ultimately be converted into positive responses. It's a matter of adopting your customers' perspective of your company—what we call taking an outside-in view of the business. Often, this discussion can spark new opportunities to serve that market and accelerate growth in an untapped industry or customer segment.

- **Rule #4: Customize the Road Map for Each Customer.** Companies love to draw "road maps" that tell the market where they want to go with their products and services. But often what's missing from these strategy documents is an assessment of where your *customers* want to go. A better type of road map is one that charts the journey that you and your customer are *taking together.* These customer-centric road maps address the special challenges each customer faces. To figure out the best road map for a given customer, companies should do more "strategic planning"—consultive engagements whose main purpose is to gain an understanding of the customer's specific goals and constraints, and to brainstorm different approaches to a problem. In these engagements, product sales are purposely left off the table in favor of building trust and fleshing out smart strategies. This kind of personalized "road-mapping" will help your company stand out in a congested marketplace, showing customers that it's not just about pushing products and closing deals. Oracle, as one example, has created and deployed a "Global Client Advisor" role, with the primary responsibility of developing these roadmaps on a full-time basis with its top customers.

Customer engagement should start well before the first sale and continue long afterward. Long-term industry leadership can be built only on enduring and trusting customer relationships.

Professional Services: Going Beyond Implementation

Professional services teams are often the unheralded workhorses of your company, providing the "blocking and tackling" that clears the way for a successful product installation, technology implementation, and the like. The team's goal usually is to get the product up and running, and make the customer happy, before departing for the next job.

We believe the Subscription Economy will allow professional services to play a more strategic role in the enterprise. In fact, we've talked to leaders who are now differentiating themselves by transforming professional services teams from primarily onsite implementers, engineers, and installers into "trusted advisors" that can help enrich the customer relationship and spark long-term loyalty and deeper investments.

Professional services teams are ideally positioned to accept the bigger role. No other group ventures deeper into the trenches of your customer's operations than professional services. Team members almost always come away with insights that can be surprisingly useful to the relationship, including strategies for making your product even more valuable to the business, such as by further integrating it with other systems.

In fact, becoming a trusted advisor is really the logical next step for professional services. Since they have hands-on knowledge about how to predict and remove implementation barriers—both technical and organizational—your services teams can provide the assurances that embolden your customers to embark on a major transformational journey.

Honesty Breeds Trust

At a recent executive conference we co-hosted, many executives observed that their true strategic partners were the ones that were honest about assessing the market. These partners were willing to concede their competitors' edge in specific areas and even recommending competitive products when it was to the advantage of the customer. We have yet to see a situation where this doesn't pay off in the long run.

Customer Service: From Break-Fix to Business Outcomes

We believe that customer service and support organizations will be flipped on their heads. The traditional call centers of the past will be reinvented to become "customer success centers" that spend less time addressing product and service complaints and more time optimizing business outcomes.

The Internet of Things and the cloudification of business, trends we explored in Chapter 1, "Two Meta Trends Shaping the Competition," are driving the transition. The modern customer service operation connects to a huge volume of information, including streams of data from sensors embedded in the products themselves. This level of connectivity provides real-time performance monitoring and the capability to solve problems without the customer ever knowing that the problem existed. The ability to minimize customer incidents will allow these teams to spend more time helping customers fully realize business outcomes.

Table 5.1 shows the major shifts we see happening to customer service and support organizations.

Table 5.1 Shifting Focus in Customer Service and Support Organizations

From	To
Support generally focuses on specific product issues, from a technical perspective.	More focus on cross-product issues and whether the overall solution is properly supporting the customer's use cases and business processes.
A majority of customer activity is generated from customer-initiated support cases filed by product.	Customer activity is more focused on implementing automatic triggers embedded in the product and other forms of proactive intervention.
A majority of customer support performance measures are related to case resolution time and service level agreements.	A majority of customer success performance measures are related to customer retention and business outcome results.

We're witnessing the first stages of the transformation of customer services, the success of which will depend on companies deploying a range of "listening posts" to capture, analyze, and act on customer feedback. Oracle, for example, is using persistent connections to its engineered systems products to know when and how to add capacity, patch software, and anticipate issues before they become a problem. The efficiency and effectiveness of these real-time service engagements will add "stickiness" to your relationship and, moreover, spur add-on sales.

Product Development: Turning Products into Customer Success

It goes without saying that product development, or R&D, is a critical function of any enterprise. Revenue and profitability rely on customers buying (or subscribing to) a product that works as advertised and delivers measurable value. Product developers that fail this basic test—especially the value delivery part—will soon find themselves the object of intense scrutiny by executives, boards, and investors. In many ways, it's your product that embodies your brand and determines the fate of your business.

Ironically, though, product development organizations are often the last to join what we call the "customer success journey"—to strategically engage customers. There are many reasons for this, of course: Product engineers are often revered in many organizations, creating an "ivory tower" mentality; R&D teams too often adopt a build-it-and-they-will-come approach, exposing the company to being blindsided by abrupt market changes; and executive in-fighting can often prevent product developers from effectively collaborating—both with each other and with other parts of the business.

With the advent of the Internet of Things and the Subscription Economy, it's more important than ever for companies to rethink their R&D plans to take advantage of emerging business models and technology platforms. We feel strongly that companies can capture these trends, and the revenue opportunities associated with them, only when product development teams take a seat at the table next to others in your enterprise who are strategically engaging the customer.

From factory machines to automobiles to networking equipment, nearly every product will be touched by the next wave of customer success innovation. As a result, the traditional approach of relegating product development to the back office or lab will be supplanted by *co-development*, where vendors and customers work together to develop the next generation of features or products. This strategy will require tight integration with sales and marketing teams to leverage the insights they're gathering from customers. Product development teams will also need to work more closely with customer service and other operational teams to ensure that products—now increasingly delivered as a service—are actually being used by your customer and fulfilling business value promises.

By adopting a co-development approach, companies will swiftly incorporate feedback from all their teams and systems into next-generation designs with the goal of further improving business outcomes and customer success. In many cases, the feedback loop and subsequent tweaks will be unknown to the customer. Rockwell Automation, for example, now designs its machines with IoT-enabled sensors so that the company can monitor its machines and fix them automatically at a distance. This lets Rockwell's customers focus on production schedules and throughput instead of machine upkeep. Once more we are seeing the transition to outcomes-based customer engagements, in this case enabled by forward-thinking product developers.

We believe there are three new engagement capabilities for customer success-driven product development organizations:

- **Collaborative Product Road Maps.** For years, most product development road maps—planning documents that set forth the expected direction of future products—have taken into account customer insights from customer surveys, third-party research, and focus groups. These methods supply important feedback, helping engineers fix product flaws and prioritize new "features and functions." In the Subscription Economy, however, product development must think more holistically—for example, by anticipating changing industry conditions and how they will impact the kinds of business outcomes customers will desire. The answers to these questions may push developers to completely reimagine the products they build. For your most strategic customers, we advocate the use of co-development product road map techniques. We present a great example of a company that has instituted a co-development process with its customers in our profile of the cloud-logistics innovator Telogis in Chapter 4. The ability for Telogis to synch its product strategy with its customers has been a major driver of the company's overwhelming success over the past six-plus years.

Tied at the Hip

A well-developed long-range product road-mapping process is a win-win for you and your customers. As you understand more about your customers' long-term strategy, your engineering teams can design a road map to match. Co-development adds validity and longevity to the relationship, ensuring that the two companies are "tied at the hip" for years to come.

- **IoT Enablement.** As we've pointed out elsewhere, IoT-enabled products provide huge opportunities for engaging with your customer more strategically. Connecting formerly "stand-alone" products (and services) to the Internet is becoming a big part of more product road maps, not least because it enables a key driver of customer success: real-time performance monitoring of products in the field. IoT enablement requires R&D teams to change the way they plan and invest in future products. Leveraging big data and analytic tools helps accelerate product innovation and time to market.

- **Quarterly Business Reviews.** These regular check-ins with customers are one of the key routines for account managers worldwide. To fully engage strategically with your customers, however, we recommend adding product developers to these sales-led customer update and planning sessions. QBRs provide valuable insights into products that are falling short of expectations or failing to integrate smoothly with the rest of the business. Involving your product developers in these meetings exposes them directly to your customer's business decision makers, adding another channel of insight, or listening post, that can be incorporated into the R&D process.

The Role of Automation in Strategic Customer Engagements

Before closing this chapter, we would be remiss if we didn't discuss the role of new technologies to help automate and scale strategic customer engagements. These are technology solutions that enable sales, marketing, and product development teams to interact more successfully with customers and each other. Global enterprises need to strategically engage with hundreds to thousands of customers and partners while coordinating the efforts of its far-flung sales, marketing, service, and product development teams. The good news is that a number of new technologies already exist to support these endeavors, including these:

- **Sales Enablement Platforms.** These solutions provide ROI and business-case tools to customers, partners, and sales teams. The cloud-based versions of these tools reduce distribution, data collection, updating, and reporting complexities.

- **Marketing Automation Platforms.** These solutions automate your lead-generation efforts and marketing campaigns across a full range of channels, including e-mail and social media. The tools streamline key tasks such as audience segmentation, persona development, communications scheduling, and campaign tracking.

- **Content Management Platforms.** These solutions provide a repository and management framework for content editors and development teams. Designed with "content marketing" programs in mind, these platforms reduce content-development efforts and automate distribution and impact reporting.

Engaging the Whole Organization

Tips for becoming a strategically engaged enterprise:

Marketing

- Widen your focus beyond just generating customer awareness and buzz.

- Track and promote your solution's business outcomes throughout the customer lifecycle.

- Shift more marketing dollars from presales to retention-oriented programs.

- Establish strategic relationships that identify new market opportunities and thought leadership.

- Implement a segmentation and customer engagement strategy.

Sales

- Look beyond just closing deals and hitting short-term sales quota targets.

- Think bigger: Ask your sales teams how many of them are calling on technical and functional executive-level decision makers today.

- Add a cadre of expert resources who know your customers' industries and are able to relate customer futures to your product road map.

Professional Services

- Shift the perception of professional services from "necessary evil" to "trusted advisor."

- Move teams from focusing solely on product deployment to creating strategic road maps for customers.

- Build relationships beyond tech users to business leaders.

- Ask how you can drive your customers' success over the next three to five years through unique consultative engagements.

Customer Service and Support

- Become proactive through the use of IoT-enabled technologies.

- Ask your customer service leaders what new listening posts they have on their road map.

- Ask whether these new capabilities are providing a quantum leap in service levels over the past.

Product Development

- Shift from thinking features and functions to thinking how your product can deliver specific business outcomes.

- Take advantage of IoT capabilities and the quantum leap in customer insights captured from "listening posts."

Strategic customer engagement will have a profound effect on core business functions: sales, support, service, marketing, and product development. Marketing is in a unique position to take a leadership role in defining the customer lifecycle and designing an engagement program that is consistent, comprehensive, and ultimately delivers the long-term, strategic relationships that customers are clamoring for.

We now turn to look at a company that has made engaging the customer strategically a core part of its corporate DNA.

Endnotes

[1] "The Value of Customer Experience, Quantified," Peter Kriss, *Harvard Business Review*, August 2014.

[2] Based on interviews with Andy Monshaw, former COO of IBM Japan and Executive Partner at Siris Capital Group.

6

Cisco: Engaging Customers to Deliver Business Outcomes

"Market transitions wait for no one."

—John Chambers

In recent years, few companies have integrated customer success as part of their go-to-market DNA better than Internet pioneer Cisco. Founded in 1984 by Leonard Bosack and Sandy Lerner, Cisco has been riding the Internet wave for more than three decades, supplying businesses with the plumbing that runs the Web—the switches, routers, and networking gear that shuttle information between computers around the world. In 1991, Cisco hired John Chambers, who took Cisco from a $1 billion networking company to one of the most admired global technology leaders.

It's no surprise that Cisco's success attracted a crowd of upstarts and innovators eager to grab a share of the $19 trillion Internet of Things (IoT) market (or, as Cisco calls it, the Internet of Everything market).

The San Jose, California company has fended off competitive threats with an ambitious market transition strategy, simultaneously broadening its product portfolio to capture high-growth opportunities and shedding lines of business that didn't play to the company's strengths as it—and the industry—evolved. Thus, Cisco branched into unified computing, cloud computing, and collaboration solutions (with its acquisition of WebEx) while also spinning off a line of non-core consumer products (home automation, home routing, IP-based video cameras).

But an even bigger challenge had been looming for Cisco and all high tech players: The buying process changed, and no longer were the buyers of IT product-driven; rather, they had become business-centric and outcome-driven. And if vendors can't meet the new requirements of the customer's buying process, they risk being marginalized. Cisco clearly heard customers asking tough questions such as, "How will this help me compete more effectively, build better products, or innovate faster?" Increasingly, Cisco's customers wanted to know how the tech giant was going to help them achieve positive business outcomes.

Executives at Cisco took notice, quickly coming to the realization that if the company didn't start changing the nature of its customer relationships from product-centric to customer success-centric, demand for its products and services would cool, and customers might be lured to other suppliers. Cisco wanted to make sure that it did a better job of communicating and delivering business outcomes to customers in areas that mattered, such as revenue growth, profitability, customer loyalty, and competitiveness. So a few years ago the company green-lighted a major overhaul of the way Cisco "goes to market." Leading the effort was Sandy Hogan, Senior Vice President of the Business Transformation Group (BTX) at Cisco, a position she holds today. Hogan's charter was clear: Reinvent how the company engages and interacts with its customers. The new focus of Cisco's customer relationships would center firmly around business outcomes. "We want to help our customers realize the value of everything they are investing in for the future of their business," Hogan tells us.

To do this, Cisco decided to buck traditional ways of marketing and selling, and tap into the expertise of champions like Hogan and her team. They were tasked to fundamentally change how the organization goes to market. The goal: drive the delivery of integrated strategies that enable business outcomes and ensure that customers realize the full value of their technology investments. Hogan's transformation team includes both vertical and enterprise capabilities, a structure designed to fully integrate products, services, partners, and support. Acting like a start-up, BTX reflects deep industry knowledge, bridges business and IT strategy, and is designed to increase customer intimacy and deliver business outcomes.

For Hogan and her team, success would be all about communicating, demonstrating, and ensuring that Cisco solutions deliver business outcomes that matter to its customers. "Only by effectively engaging and partnering with the customer to deliver on expected outcomes can you build the level of trust and loyalty needed to sustain market leadership over the long haul," Hogan says. To a great extent, this was dictated by the fact that customers are struggling to deal with multiple technologies and fast-changing trends simultaneously. Hogan calls them "technology transitions," and they include everything from the complexities of big data to the spread of social media and mobile devices into the workplace to the unavoidable need to identify and mitigate the growing cyber-security threats.

For the average customer, this means that no single product can help them solve all of their technology challenges. For Cisco, these technology transitions called into question its long-standing strategy of selling individual products that provide specific, discrete capabilities. For example, Telepresence products provide a HD-quality voice and video experience. Without a business application, these products can be viewed as a novelty or an expensive tech toy—sold in "silos," as Hogan says. She has been urging Cisco to ask: "How do you solve for the customer's complex range of needs—and then understand and measure whether you're accomplishing what was promised." In other words, "the focus should not be on *what* you're selling, but on *how* you're selling and how you are delivering."

Culture Shift

To achieve its goal of outcome-oriented engagements, Cisco launched a major investment in fundamentally changing its sales organization. Every aspect from employee roles and responsibilities to compensation would be reevaluated. Hogan hired people from outside Cisco to bring a fresh perspective to the selling process. "We drove a huge transformation and took a very strategic approach to building our team," Hogan says.

Of course, you might expect that switching from a focus on selling products to delivering "outcomes" while maintaining quotas would come as a culture shock to its sales reps. Cisco is asking everyone to play an active role and adopt a new mind-set. "We have to continuously push the system," Hogan says. "We needed to make it a little uncomfortable. Business as usual is no longer good enough." For Cisco, it's really not about doing it one way or the other. It's about doing both—quotas are fine and selling the components is fine, but you *also* have to provide the context. Meaning Cisco people have to tell the whole story from beginning to end and then deliver to customers and ensure outcomes within that context.

Cisco's new "go to market" model fully embraces the customer's point of view, asking in effect, "how do we change our organization to align to their business imperatives?" Compensation structures are being fine-tuned so that they're "not so tactically focused," and the company is adding longer-term customer success goals into compensation plans aimed at getting sales teams to adopt outcomes-oriented behaviors. Hogan describes the new structure as "more empowerment and less control," whereby corporate management becomes the coach and the account manager is the quarterback and the overall strategist, the result of which is a reduction in bottlenecks and enhanced collaboration with the customer on the business outcome that has been targeted. All this enables much closer customer alignment.

Cisco's fresh focus on business outcomes is still a work in progress, but the company has taken concrete steps toward making it a reality. For example, BTX is testing a concept called the "Business Value Framework" designed to help Cisco's sales teams define "everything the customer is trying to solve for"—such as enabling a new business capability—and then aligning everybody in a coordinated effort to design and deliver the overall solution.

Account managers are encouraged to mobilize all of Cisco's assets (e.g., industry experts, technical architects, executive leadership, business consultants) and to "share goals" across this larger team. This new collaborative approach allows for greater focus on the customer and less emphasis on particular products. To encourage adoption, BTX has created and rolled out what it calls a "Business Outcome Approach," which drives consistency across teams, sets rules for engaging resources, and establishes milestones that will show progress toward meeting the customer's desired business results.

The Language of Business Outcomes

Restructuring sales teams to focus on customer outcomes is only one aspect of Cisco's overall strategy. Another important facet includes helping customers understand the business impact they should expect from their technology investment—and following up with metrics that showcase the actual impact on the business after the sale.

To help customers understand the full potential of an investment and buy into and promote the benefits they're likely to see, Hogan's team uses the business outcome approach (see Figure 6.1) to define the engagement process at different stages of the customer journey. By hiring and sourcing an ecosystem of business value and industry experts, BTX has created a team that helps guide customers to identify, assess, measure, and deliver on the business impacts of Cisco's solutions.

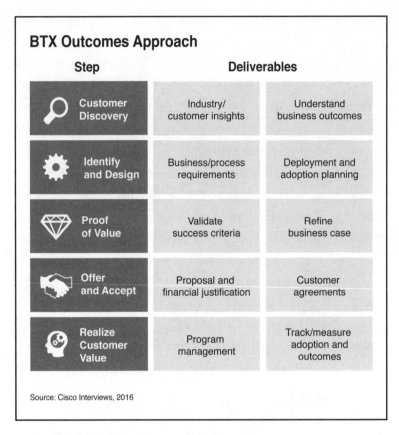

Figure 6.1 Cisco's business outcomes approach.

In recent years, Cisco has conducted in-depth projections of business outcomes at dozens of companies in different sectors (see the call out box, "How Cisco Engaged a Retail Chain with Business Outcomes Focus," for one example). Notably Cisco offers customers an ability to independently estimate business outcomes through a set of online business-value tools that draw from industry benchmarks and business results gathered from the experiences of hundreds of companies. But do these forecasts pan out? Are they accurate? Hogan says they take an extra step by sponsoring "post-implementation studies"—especially involving the same customers that participated in the earlier forecasts—to "close the loop" on Cisco's promise of business results.

Turning the Tide

All of this points to the day when Cisco not only sells the promise of business outcomes but actually ties fees to delivering these outcomes. What it comes down to, Hogan says, is having "skin in the game." Ultimately, customer success is this: "How do we all have a stake in the game as to how outcomes are delivered in the customer environment?"

Cisco still has work to do, executives explain, but such outcomes-based revenue models may become a real possibility in the years ahead. In the meantime, Cisco wants the delivery of business outcomes to become a "repeatable objective" that is both predictable and accountable. In other words, if "you implement these three solutions, this is what you should be able to accomplish," Hogan says.

Cisco is convinced that supporting customer success, from opportunity identification to delivery of business outcomes, will create real differentiation for the company. After all, customers are demanding it for good reason. "When you think about it, software, hardware, the cloud: those are just a means to achieving something more important," Hogan says. "Customers will get to a point where they won't make investments unless they have predictability of what the outcome will be." This will likely increase Cisco's service capabilities in the market. Cisco's recent financial results indicate that this thinking is on track. Cisco Services' revenue increased for the 49th consecutive quarter to $2.9 billion, making up 22.9% of total Cisco revenue.

Newly appointed CEO Chuck Robbins indicates that the company will continue to acquire software and security firms and transition pricing to the subscription and SaaS models that customers are demanding. With that guidance, the 21% increase in deferred revenue in fiscal year 2015 speaks to the seriousness of Cisco's transition that Hogan is leading.

How Cisco Engaged a Retail Chain with Business Outcomes Focus

One specialty retailer is replacing its voice communications platform in its stores and corporate headquarters with a Cisco collaboration solution. This investment was developed through a series of executive briefings and workshops provided by an integrated team of Cisco retail specialists, system engineers, solution architects, and account team members. Initial discussions were not about products; rather they focused on the business outcomes of deploying a collaboration capability in a retail environment.

The team worked hand in hand with the company's IT organization, meeting with key business leaders to capture nearly 40 business use cases that demonstrate how a collaboration solution could help move the needle on the company's corporate strategy—increasing revenue, enhancing customer experiences, improving store associate and management productivity, and creating a platform to enable new omni-channel service capabilities.

Highlighting the limitations of its current technology and the advantages of the Cisco solution, the retailer was able to better grasp the strategic, operational, and financial impacts of the new solution.

The business outcomes-oriented program was presented to the retailer's board of directors and enabled the company to properly weigh its capital investment options (e.g., implementing a collaboration solution versus marketing, HR, or supply chain investments).

The customer engagement included the following steps:

- **Strategic goal alignment.** Identifying strategic goals that could be impacted by collaboration across key functional areas: merchandising, store operations, supply chain/distribution, corporate/executive management, IT management, e-commerce, marketing, human resources, digital, product development.

- **Business use case development.** Researching key business functions and interviewing key members of management to uncover challenges with current business processes. Discussing collaboration-enabled business best practices to develop business use cases (e.g., how the end customers' experience with the retailer improves, how store associate efficiencies improve, how stores better comply with planogram requirements, and how much effort will it take to realize the business results).

- **Impact quantification and prioritization of business use cases.** Bringing the solution to life by measuring existing business process performance and estimating the improvements brought about by collaboration, then prioritizing use cases based on value attainment and ease of implementation.

- **Creation of a full ROI model and strategic plan for the customer.** Integrating the business strategy, use cases, and financial model to provide a 360-degree view of the investment profile. The strategic plan is then used as a tool to assess the customer's realization of value and investment performance after project approval.

Cisco's Tips for Turning Engagements into Outcomes

To effectively engage with customers, Cisco's BTX team is focusing customer engagements on business outcomes. Following are some of the principles they are following along this journey:

- **Move from a product orientation to a customer outcome orientation.** Instead of looking at individual technical capabilities, such as data center assets and technical services, Cisco looks at the customer's business challenges, including how to improve customer experiences and how to bring a new "Internet of Everything" revenue model to life.

- **Widen your scope.** Include multiple product areas, capabilities, and business areas—all with the achievement of business outcomes in mind.

- **Embrace a longer timeframe.** Achieving business outcomes takes longer than closing any given deal. So be patient. Long-term plans eventually turn into short-term opportunities.

- **Build a team that truly believes.** Most important, you have to bring in the right people that are passionately driven to deliver outcomes that matter to customers. Hogan's team has spent a tremendous amount of time securing talent, identifying competencies, and building training programs, to create a culture that withstands the ups and downs of such a transformation.

7

Ensure

"Some of us will do our jobs well and some will not, but we will be judged by only one thing: the result."

—Vince Lombardi

How do you deliver business outcomes in the Customer First Revolution? We have proposed that it takes three critical capabilities working in tandem to deliver outcomes that matter to customers and, in so doing, empower you to outcompete rivals in the Subscription Economy.

Comprehensive listening is the first of these capabilities and the foundation for the other two, providing visibility into what customers really need and what makes them successful in their markets and business ecosystems. Second, we've proposed that you need to harness the intelligence gathered from proactive listening to engage customers in a deeply strategic fashion, a process that extends well past the close of any given sale. These strategic engagements are a necessary part of building a *trusted advisor* relationship that helps drive retention and revenue growth.

Effective listening and engaging alone are not enough to deliver success for your customers—and in turn your business—over the long term. You also need to *ensure* that you are delivering outcomes that will actually impact your customers' business. It is this third capability—the ability of companies to prove they are in fact living up to their promises—that we'll explore in this chapter.

The Most Critical Capability

Our experience shows that the ability to *ensure* business outcomes is the most important of the three capabilities, and it is the hardest to master. No matter how well you listen to your customers, or how intimately you engage with them, if you fail to deliver meaningful business results, sooner or later customers will gravitate to vendors that can.

Ensuring business outcomes is fundamentally about sticking around after the sale, paying attention to what creates results and providing customer programs that increase the likelihood that expected business outcomes will be achieved. Ask yourself, what do the first 90 days look like after your customer "goes live" with your products? A lot can happen during that time, both good and bad, that can influence whether customers will be successful in using and deriving value from your products. More specifically, renewal revenues are in great part driven by customer adoption and usage. Getting over the initial hump and ensuring an extended period of benefits realization by aligning with your customer's business is, to a large extent, how you drive loyalty and high retention rates.

Recall that in the upside-down world of the Subscription Economy, companies generally don't start making money until their customers renew subscriptions several times over. So it's essential to employ strategies and techniques that help ensure customer success over an extended period of time. It's not enough to wish for it. The whole point of deploying *ensure* capabilities as part of your customer success strategy is that—if executed correctly—they will allow you to consistently deliver outcomes that you've defined in the course of your listening and engagement activities.

Another lesson of the Subscription Economy is that customer relationships should necessarily encompass a longer time horizon. As we observed earlier in this book, most B2B organizations focus exclusively on getting new customers in the door—a laudable goal, but hardly a guarantee of sustainable growth in an economy that more and more runs on renewals. In truth, we've seen only a handful of companies that are making a real effort at ensuring that their customers' business objectives are being met. Two of these enterprises are profiled in the next chapters; not coincidentally, both are leading their respective industries in growth, innovation, and profitability.

To consistently deliver customer success, companies need to adopt a *holistic approach* that engages every part of the organization over the entire customer lifecycle. By doing so, each of these organizations will transform themselves into modern customer success-oriented operations, and become highly competitive in the process.

Marketing, for example, will generate more leads by informing its campaigns with business outcomes and success metrics. Sales organizations will see heftier renewal commissions when they become more engaged in post-sales product adoption and business results. Likewise, engineering teams that focus on engineering *outcomes* rather than mere features will discover new markets never before imagined.

Ironically, modern professional services and support teams may be in the best position to guarantee day-to-day business results. These are the people who are most intimately connected to the inner workings of customers and best able to instill confidence in the B2B seller's products and services. Bucking the tradition of playing second fiddle to sales and engineering, these teams are becoming the new champions of customer success and the new drivers of retention and revenue in the Subscription Economy.

The bottom line is that every single part of the organization will need to gear itself toward ensuring customer success by delivering outcomes. To that end, we see companies developing a new set of capabilities tailored to helping customers achieve the full potential of business value in every product and service they purchase (or subscribe to). We group these vendor-supplied services into three categories:

1. Adoption optimization
2. Customer performance measurement
3. Value measurement and realization

The authors currently are working with organizations worldwide to help them deliver precisely these services to customers and in the process reach a new level of competitiveness. Let's take a closer look.

Adoption Optimization

If you're seeking to ensure that your customers achieve business outcomes, you should start by making sure your customers are actually adopting your products and using them to their maximum advantage. That's the goal of what we call *adoption optimization* services, and it's what more companies are rolling out in the Subscription Economy.

It goes without saying that usage patterns will vary according to the type of product or service being used—but we've found that most vendors can adequately define a target adoption level, including a recommended number of active users and the specific product features they should be using. To maximize impact, adoption efforts should start early—even before the product is delivered or "goes live"—and continue indefinitely as new users come onboard and new features are added.

In setting the adoption agenda with customers, we have found that the first three months after deployment are the most critical; that's when both the customer and the provider are the most keenly motivated and engaged. As illustrated in Figure 7.1, 90% of a company's loyal customers are secured in the first 97 days. This is also exactly the right time to develop a multiyear plan to ensure adoption well beyond this crucial initial stage.

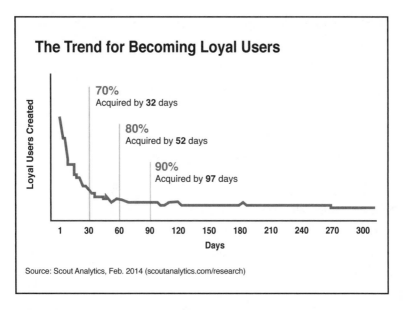

Figure 7.1 Adoption patterns of loyal users.

Here's a summary of what a good adoption optimization program should include:

- **Adoption planning** to forecast the optimal usage of the solution to be deployed, linked clearly to targeted business outcomes

- **Onboarding services** to train new users, not just on features and functions but also on business-process improvements

- **Marketing and communications** to promote early successes or "wins" and build excitement and awareness around the new product

- **Forums**, both internal to the customer organization and outside, for exploring best practices and lessons learned

- **User groups and workshops** to target project "champions" and power users who can then encourage others to adopt the solution as well as provide recommendations for improving the solution

- **Change management services** to remove barriers to adoption that may arise due to cultural, process, or organizational inertia
- **Consumption monitoring** to track the actual use of the product and motivate laggards. (New cloud technologies generally allow companies to track usage of products automatically and in real time.)

Adoption and usage data may not be perfect evidence that a customer is realizing value from a product, but it's a good leading indicator. Moreover, adoption statistics can be used to help companies better tailor marketing and promotional campaigns aimed at new and existing customers.

Customer Performance Measurement

Think of adoption as the first step toward delivering business outcomes. Next is *measuring the performance* of customers after they start using your products. Of course, this assumes you *know* what constitutes good and bad performance and how to measure it. Many of the companies we studied worked with their customers to define key business performance indicators (KPIs) and then implemented a performance measurement plan to continuously monitor and manage these targets. Doing so allowed customers to measure actual performance against the full potential of a particular business process—say, opportunity management, supply chain management, services delivered—or even the business as a whole.

Naturally, there is a difference between measuring performance and actually delivering full-potential outcomes. In the information technology industry, for example, Gartner estimates that companies are achieving only 43% of their technology investments' full potential value.[1] But we have found that an effective performance measurement and monitoring system—one that is simple, transparent, and truly reflects the customer's value-creation processes—provides the engine for continually refining joint business goals, and the product itself, to increase the likelihood of successful outcomes.

A modern performance measurement system should help you do the following:

- **Identify and measure key business processes.** The system should be able to select and monitor the most critical business processes and capture the data source, individual responsible, and frequency of measurement.

- **Capture benchmarks and best practices.** The system should be able to track actual business performance against benchmarks and document best practices within customer operations (thus helping new departments, business units, and customers bypass common pitfalls when rolling out products).

- **Automate and centralize measurement processes.** The system should be able to speed data capture and analysis and make it possible to embed performance management features into product installations.

Of course not all measures are created equal, so it's vital for business leaders to be discerning about the kinds of performance measures that would make sense in different customer situations. Broadly speaking, these metrics cover a range of categories and may be roughly split into operational, financial, and strategic measures. Operational metrics focus on measures of efficiency. Financial metrics look at revenue, overhead costs, profit margins, and the like. Strategic measures, though harder to define and track, focus on areas such as market share, customer experience, and brand awareness.

A comprehensive performance measurement system would ideally incorporate all three types of measures to gauge the overall success of a customer deploying your products and services. In practice, performance measurement can be a delicate balancing act. Many companies either measure the right things but don't do a good job of actually measuring and tracking them, or measure too many things, some of which aren't relevant. The latter is especially true for online services and Internet-connected products that allow for measuring a slew of things that weren't measureable in the past, including usage, adoption, and machine performance.

To make sense of the mix, it helps to spend time understanding exactly how the different measures relate to each other, and—crucially—how different individuals and teams in your company, such as sales, marketing, R&D, and support, play a role in influencing these different types of outcomes. Thus, when you work with customers to create a performance measurement system, consider the following guidelines that we have found to be extremely helpful:

- Select just a few performance measurements and take care not to dilute your focus with too much data. It is critical to find measures that matter to the customer.

- Be relentless about determining what performance measures truly matter, and make sure that those performance measures are linked to the strategic priorities of the company. We invariably focus on the three performance measurement categories mentioned earlier:

  - Operational: wins versus losses, product adoption, consumption of features, process cycle time improvements, on-time attainment of key milestones, subscription renewal rates, service requests logged, system uptime compared to service level agreements

  - Financial: customer focused: time to benefits, incremental value realized; company: revenue and margins, annual renewal revenue, annual churn

  - Strategic: customer satisfaction and loyalty, referenceability, level of active referencing, overall customer health, market share, share of wallet

- Create performance measurement systems that are rigorous. A system is disciplined when the measurement and review processes are applied consistently and fairly on a regular basis and when "gaming the system" is minimized.

- Revisit these performance measurements every few quarters to prevent them from becoming stale or obsolete. It is amazing how long companies can go without questioning the validity and relevance of the numbers they use to manage the business.

- Build a fact-based system of performance measurement, and be comfortable setting stretch goals. (In most companies, target setting can be pure gamesmanship.)

- Work with metrics that are easily understood and communicated, so that your organization, and the customer's, are best equipped to digest and actually consume and respond to the information presented.

Ultimately, a customer success dashboard that has been collaboratively developed with key stakeholders (sales, marketing, service, customers, etc.) can be a useful tool to track trends and provide a factual basis for taking remedial actions. Just as important, a dashboard can become a vehicle to communicate the overall impact of customer success programs.

Value Tree Approach to Performance Measurement

When we work with companies to help them understand and create a consensus for desired business outcomes, we often like to develop a *value tree*—a business logic framework that breaks down the company's goals, areas for improvement, and metrics—allowing the customer to focus on what truly matters and identifying which elements of the business solution are most important.

In developing a value tree, we look at three aspects of value impact:

- **Value Categories.** Include impact areas such as profitability, revenue, risk mitigation, OPEX savings, or CAPEX savings

- **Value Drivers.** One or more measurable impacts per value category

- **Value Benchmarks.** Cause-effect relationships and estimates of potential value for each value driver

Figure 7.2 shows an example of value tree analysis created for a leading healthcare organization.

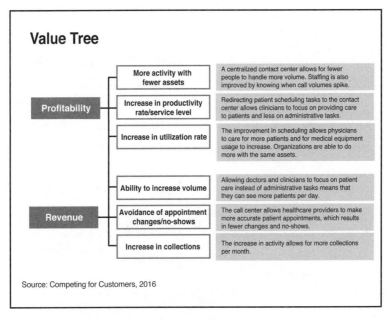

Figure 7.2 Value tree example: healthcare organization.

Value Management and Realization

Let's assume you are actively promoting adoption of your products and services, and you've designed a performance measurement system to track your customer's progress in relation to their value tree. What's left now—the missing link needed for ensuring success—is to *measure actual value realized.* We see this as the last mile of customer success because the better you can show and communicate ongoing business value realized, the more you'll be perceived not just as a vendor but as a strategic business partner.

Remember that the goal is to help your customers fully utilize and then realize maximum value from your products. That in turn will help you drive customer retention and increase revenue for *your* business. Amazingly, very few organizations focus real attention on helping customers with product adoption and realization of business benefits.

There are many ways you can demonstrate value realized, but doing it well requires that it be built into *collaborative account management* practices and a structured approach to *executive sponsorship*. Account management and executive sponsorship are discussed throughout the book, including in Chapter 11, "How Oracle Focuses on Customer Success." We place further emphasis here because we see these capabilities as foundational for customer success, and especially so for benefits realization.

The following are the core steps in establishing an effective value or benefits realization methodology:

- **Establish a collaborative account planning process.** Account planning and day-to-day execution of the plan should align your success with that of your customers.

- **Engage strong executive sponsorship.** Assigning a strong and active executive sponsor from your organization will reinforce the collaborative and "trusted advisor" nature of the relationship, account management, product adoption, and benefits realization.

- **Agree on your value proposition.** This can simply consist of a statement about how your products are going to create value and the business outcomes expected. Value propositions should be written to resonate with all key influencers, including executives, business-line leaders, and technical experts.

- **Quantify and communicate business outcomes.** List the key business areas to be impacted along with the associated financial results using the customer's internal metrics and hurdle rates. Financial results will focus on hard-dollar impacts; soft benefits should be grouped separately.

- **Validate actual value realized.** At the end of the process, hold a "close-the-loop" meeting with your customer's stakeholders in which you revisit your value proposition and present proof of the business value they've realized.

As you go through the value measurement process, try to understand how different types of stakeholders—the CEO, the CFO, the CIO, the business-unit vice president—measure success. Each one typically views the business through a slightly different lens and it's important to understand the differences. C-level executives, for example, are most often concerned with making sure the strategic vision and priorities of the company are being fulfilled. Economic stakeholders, like CFOs, concentrate on making sure the capital investment hurdle rates of the company are being met. Line-of-business managers need to make sure departmental goals are being advanced. Technical and subject-matter experts, on the other hand, may be more narrowly focused on ensuring that the technology actually works and will integrate successfully with other solutions in the business.

Collaborative account management processes and resources play a central role in ensuring that business outcomes are attained. Getting your customer to buy into a three-year account plan can make a big difference in driving strategic day-to-day engagements with a distinct focus on benefits measurement and realization, as illustrated in Figure 7.3.

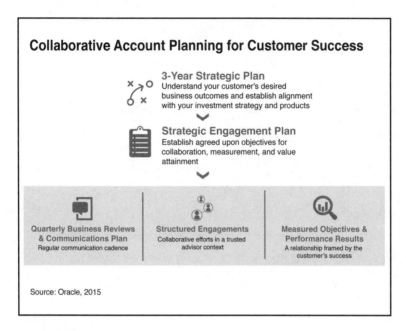

Figure 7.3 Collaboration account planning.

As illustrated in Figure 7.4, adopting a strong executive sponsorship program is another critical element of developing a trusted advisor relationship and making good on the promise of delivering value. Market leaders such as Cisco and Oracle have invested heavily in sophisticated programs to maximize the time executives spend with key customers. The executive sponsor provides a strategic resource for both the customer and the account manager, helping define the customer's business objectives and removing internal roadblocks that can prevent the customer from achieving their business outcomes.

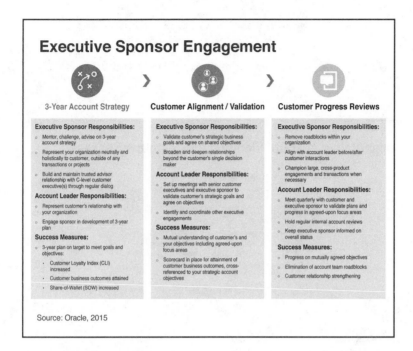

Figure 7.4 Alignment of the executive sponsor with the account team to ensure outcomes.

Showing value realization in concrete ways—and particularly in ways that align with the operational, financial, and strategic metrics you've highlighted in your customer's value tree—can be among the most important milestones of your relationship with the customer. Of course, there are always more milestones to reach and you can never let down your guard, but it is a powerful demonstration that you are indeed delivering not just a product but valuable outcomes that enable business success for the customer.

As we have said throughout this book, these wins are the direct result of adopting an integrated approach to customer success—a holistic process that builds on intelligence from careful proactive listening, which in turn defines and drives strategic engagement programs, and culminates in systematic efforts to ensure and deliver specific business outcomes.

The next two chapters examine two companies that are taking customer success seriously, to the extent of even creating new commercial models based on delivering specific business outcomes.

> ### Are You Measuring Value?
>
> More companies are making it a priority to understand, track, and communicate the actual business value their customers realize. How about you? Can you affirmatively answer the following questions about *your* company?
>
> - Are your customers truly benefiting from your products and services?
>
> - Do you measure the ROI and business impact of the top-five solutions at your top-100 customers?
>
> - Do you proactively and regularly present the value your solutions are delivering to your most important customers?

Endnote

[1] Gartner Executive Program Survey, 2013.

8

How GE Power Fuels Growth by Delivering Outcomes

When you think of a company that is breaking new ground in digital business models, GE Power may not be the first company that comes to mind. Headquartered in Schenectady, New York, Power is GE's largest industrial business, recently earning more than $27 billion in revenue from the efforts of approximately 38,000 employees serving customers in more than 125 countries.

Among other products, GE Power builds the world's most powerful and efficient gas turbine—the 9HA—a 400-ton engineering tour de force that powers the most advanced power plants around the globe. The GE division excels in many other industrial fields, from distributed power and nuclear energy to wind, water, and other renewable resource technologies. And with the recent acquisition of Alstom Power, GE's largest industrial investment to date, GE Power is accelerating its transition into a digital industrial company.

Although its roots may lie firmly in the world of industrial equipment, in recent years GE Power has learned that building great turbines is only part of what makes it successful in the eyes of customers. In recent years, it has been designing and launching innovative commercial models that seek to deliver—indeed, ensure—specific business outcomes in exchange for a share of the benefits customers realize. As an innovator in this domain, we consider GE Power to be one of the pioneers in the Customer First Revolution.

So when did this industrial giant decide to get serious about creating new business models around customer success? To get the answer to that question, we sat down with Ganesh Bell, GE's first chief digital officer and general manager of Software & Analytics for GE Power. In this position he is responsible for leading digital innovation and transformation engagements to drive business growth.

A recent arrival at GE, Bell brought a fresh perspective to the industrial powerhouse, having held leadership positions in strategy, products, engineering, and marketing across a rare mix of large industry leaders, start-ups, and fast growth companies. Recently he was executive vice president, general manager, and chief products officer at ServiceSource, where he helped transform the company to a multi-solution cloud and data services provider and the leader in recurring revenue management.

"Within energy there are a lot of different trends that we see," Bell told us. "Everything from the proliferation of gas, to mainstreaming of renewables, to distributed energy are taking off. These impact how we create both machines and digital solutions for our customers." Given his Silicon Valley pedigree, Bell has been alert to the growing importance of software—and now the cloud and big data—in the industrial sectors in which GE operates. Although GE Power wasn't born as a software company, it recognizes that software is essential to delivering value to its customers going forward.

Transformative Journey

This marks a big change from years past, when GE viewed itself mainly as a "hardware" company, the maker of giant turbines and other industrial gear for power plants, industrial companies, and water processing facilities. The change began about 20 years ago, when customers started asking whether GE could help squeeze more energy out of their existing facilities. "Therein lies the journey that we began with delivering customer outcomes," Bell says.

So GE started collecting data on its machines, measuring their performance at customer sites like power plants and wind farms. It assembled teams of technicians and consultants to fine-tune and optimize the customers' GE equipment. This was the genesis of the division's services business, now worth billions of dollars.

Customers were pleased with the efficiencies that ensued, but this success whetted their appetite for even broader performance improvements. Not only did customers want smoothly functioning equipment, but they wanted to lock in benefits at the business and enterprise level, such as lower operating costs and better financial returns from their assets. This caused GE to start looking not only at the equipment it sold them, including upgrades and repairs on individual assets, but also at all the rest of the customer's critical infrastructure. Ensuring enterprise outcomes meant moving from focusing on a single asset to focusing on the entire business of a utility, a power producer, a hospital system, an aviation company, or a transportation company.

When GE started looking at data from the customer's entire infrastructure, it found that many of the assets were being either underutilized or not used at all. And when the power division started sharing these insights with customers, customers were intrigued. "They said, 'Hey, that's great—can you monitor this additional machine for me? Can you develop a KPI around this?'" Bell says.

This touched off a series of fruitful engagements with customers— listening sessions in the parlance of *Competing for Customers*. The discussions opened the gate to a flood of insights. "We learned a lot about what our customers care about, and what makes them successful in their business," Bell says. "We found that customers wanted to move to enterprise-level outcomes. They wanted to get new insights and new value from all the data they have. And they wanted to be able to connect all those things at these different levels."

Responding to the customer outcry, GE Power set out to build out a suite of software and analytics capabilities focused on delivering customer outcomes. "We went from selling widgets to selling solutions and outcomes," Bell says. "We decided to transform our entire sales organization to solution selling and to answering the question, How do we deliver enterprise-level outcomes to our customers?"

Holistic Thinking

Bell sees the challenge as one of selling "the whole solution," a mix of hardware, services, and software assembled into an integrated package, designed to deliver specific operational and business outcomes. Solutions range from increasing performance of assets, to optimizing operations, to ultimately boosting the performance of customer revenue streams.

This is a massive change for a $27 billion company operating in 125 countries. "We're doing it at a scale that is unprecedented," Bell says. "I struggle to find examples of what others are doing on an equivalent scale, because there really are none." That's why a big part of Bell's job is to educate and rally employees to the new way of thinking.

GE's embrace of outcomes came at a time when many of its key customers—utilities, wind farm operators, and the like—faced deepening challenges, including volatile fuel prices, tighter regulations, slow demand for power growth, and an aging base of equipment.

The company's substantial size and balance sheet aided in the execution of GE's bold plan, giving it the critical mass it needed to put innovative business models into place. GE also brought to the table a wealth of proprietary expertise that traditional software companies couldn't match, including deep domain knowledge of the industries, the physical sciences, and the complex operations its customers run. What's more, it could leverage GE's leadership in the Internet of Things, or what GE calls the Industrial Internet. To bolster that effort, GE created a new division, GE Digital, featuring a software development center in the San Francisco Bay Area.

Powering Up

A few years ago, GE's wind business launched one of the company's first forays into outcomes selling. Called Wind PowerUp, this results-based platform uses GE software to increase a wind farm's output by automatically adjusting variables such as speed, torque, pitch, and aerodynamics.

When it installs the software at a wind farm, GE can guarantee an energy increase of 5%—the equivalent of adding 20 new turbines to a 400-turbine farm. Customers get the output boost they were seeking, but avoid the sizable capital outlay for new windmills. Instead, customers pay a monthly fee representing a share of the business value being delivered.

It's a great example of GE selling and delivering outcomes, not only machinery, and it's been a hit with customers for the simple fact that what customers *really* wanted to buy all along is a specific outcome: greater output from existing wind farms.

In a similar fashion, GE Power has been working with the following companies to help deliver tangible business outcomes:

- **Crestwood:** GE and this midstream oil company have embarked on an innovative software collaboration focused on productivity-enhancing asset performance management (APM). GE's APM streams asset data, decreases downtime, and enables onsite/mobile field automation tools to enable faster decisions. APM is helping Crestwood solve for business level outcomes such as uninterrupted gas gathering, enhanced performance and increased availability, compressor package visibility, and management update readiness.

- **PSEG:** Integrated energy company PSEG, in partnership with GE, is utilizing software and analytics to help generate more competitive power in its market by increasing reliability and improving operations. For the first time ever, PSEG and GE are creating enterprise business value through digital capabilities. PSEG is turning data into visibility, insights, and actions that bring improved reliability, reduced production costs, optimized asset capabilities, optimized offers, and scheduling.

- **Exelon:** Energy provider Exelon is seeing true business impact in regards to safety, cost management, and performance across its entire fleet. Driven by real business outcomes in nuclear operations, Exelon and GE are now expanding their Industrial Internet collaboration across the energy ecosystem, powered by GE's Predix.

- **RasGas:** One of the world's largest producers of liquefied natural gas, RasGas is leading the industry with a global deployment of GE's APM powered by GE's Predix platform. By effectively integrating big data and analytics, RasGas will be able to analyze the volume of machine data to improve asset utilization and performance.

Rethinking Selling

"When we talk the language of outcomes, we align with customers much more easily."

—Ganesh Bell, Chief Digital Officer, GE Power

So how do you motivate sales teams to sell software-driven outcomes rather than gas turbines? "Historically, in a hardware business we only focused on orders and revenue and contribution monitoring," Bell says. "But now we're looking at the market need and how to incentivize our sales teams very differently based on that need."

More than ever, GE is looking at the "lifetime value" of a customer, not just revenue from a single sale of equipment. "Software-enabled solutions are a different business and the metrics around them are very different," Bell says. "For example, the value of subscription revenue is different than a CAPEX-related product sale."

To get better at selling outcomes, GE is "bringing in a lot of new DNA," as Bell says, beefing up its bench with people with a background in enterprise software sales and consulting. "We're making active investments in how we build our solution selling sales force and bringing in people who can help us rethink our domain in energy. We're also retraining existing talent to the new way of thinking." GE's investment in the Industrial Internet is spearheaded by the GE Digital Center. This global innovation hub is centered in San Ramon, California (1,000 people and growing), and is backed by 10,000 software professionals from across GE's businesses around the world.

As GE explores more outcomes-based commercial models, it will need to draw from the experience of its services division, which keeps a customer's equipment running smoothly anywhere in the world. The company also will leverage its tradition of forging close, enduring relationships with customers, many of which have invested millions in large-scale industrial operations running GE equipment.

According to Bell, "GE has been really good at not just acquiring customers but actually understanding and building a relationship with customers around what matters to them. This is a great asset to build upon as we transition to this new world of selling outcomes."

To ensure great results, GE will need to monitor the full portfolio of assets that a customer owns, pulling in data from the whole infrastructure via the cloud to run analytics and provide meaningful insights into its customers' assets and operations.

Not all the assets managed will be GE branded, but all will play a role in achieving the operational or business objectives the customer seeks, such as lower costs, reduced downtime energy efficiency, or greater power output. Instead of selling assets to customers, GE is now more interested in the performance of the customer's assets.

Although selling better rotor performance to a wind farm does not have to be subscription based, GE expects more of its business models to resemble the software-as-a-service marketplace, where vendors place a premium on tracking whether and how customers adopt and use a product. It expects to become conversant in metrics such as churn rates, adoption levels, and customer success delivery. These are indicators of future revenue potential, Bell says, and these are skills that GE is currently investing in. GE is "adding a new muscle around this capability and new ways of measuring," he says. "It is part of the digital transformation we are going through."

Future of Outcomes Selling

As GE Power has proven with its PowerUp and other software-driven solutions, the market for selling business outcomes is now well established, at least at the level of an individual machine, like a gas turbine, or a collection of assets, like a wind farm. "PowerUp is a mainstream product for us, as is Asset Performance Management and Operations Optimization," Bell says. Outcomes selling at this level is now "well entrenched."

Let's be clear though: Coaxing more power out of a power plant or wind farm is one thing; guaranteeing more market share or bigger profits is quite another. Both are desirable outcomes, but it's no surprise the latter is harder to ensure—and harder to sell. Still, Bell predicts the market for such "enterprise-level outcomes" will only be a matter of time. Before that happens, though, he sees an intermediate stage taking shape in which customers connect their entire operating infrastructure—every power plant and wind farm—through the cloud, moving one step closer to full enterprise-level visibility and ensuring outcomes.

Software-defined services will likely play an even larger role in this digitally powered future. GE's recent Digital Wind Farm solution, for example, uses advanced software to individually customize each turbine to take maximum advantage of its position on the landscape. Then it connects each turbine to industrial Internet applications that continually monitor, self-learn, and fine-tune the machines to get progressively more output over time.

These initiatives show that while GE Power may not have been "born in the cloud," the company's embrace of digital transformation is rapidly transforming the way it engages with customers. "Any business going through a digital transformation and creating digital solutions is going to have to reevaluate everything from how you sell the solution, to how you measure success," Bell says. "Now that you sold them a bigger outcome, you need to be able to deliver success on a bigger scale."

Aligning with the Customer

Ready to sell business results? First you'll need to understand the outcomes—or key performance indicators (KPIs)—that matter most to your customers. That's what Ganesh Bell, GE's chief digital officer, discovered when his group adopted a version of author Eric Ries's "lean start-up" methodology to quickly develop new software for customers.

Since the rapid iterative process called for early validation of prototypes, Bell's team engaged in frequent feedback sessions with customers. "We basically went to executives and asked what are the KPIs they care about, and what are the business outcomes they're trying to drive."

To Bell's surprise, the executives were more than eager to open up. Not infrequently, executives revealed very specific details, such as performance targets that the CEO holds them accountable for.

One executive even shared his bonus plan, minus the exact dollars. "It was fascinating to see the amount of radical transparency customers have when you start talking to them about the outcomes they have to deliver," Bell says.

Bell's team seeks to integrate these KPIs into the products and dashboards GE builds for customers, ensuring full alignment and creating the infrastructure necessary for delivering business outcomes that matter to them.

9

How Rockwell Automation
Measures Success

Rockwell Automation may have been born in the age of the Model T, but it has grown and prospered in the age of the Tesla. The Milwaukee-based industrial automation company pioneered many of the key technologies that have powered the industrial age, introducing—in 1904—one of the world's first motor controllers for industrial cranes. In the century that followed, Rockwell launched thousands of electromechanical products, from the rheostats inside radios to the programmable logic controllers that orchestrate the world's assembly lines.

Although Rockwell's early devices may be worthy of a display case in the Smithsonian, the Rockwell Automation of today is more akin to a Silicon Valley start-up than a smokestack-era manufacturer. Indeed, a hefty share of its revenue comes from designing sophisticated software that governs the newest generation of automation and information systems in markets such as consumer packaged goods, food and beverage, transportation, and oil and gas.

So what can this maker of industrial control systems teach us about competing for customers? Given its old-school roots, you might not think Rockwell would be the best example of a modern customer-centric enterprise. Think again. "Rockwell is a very customer-intimate company," says Sujeet Chand, Rockwell Automation's chief technology officer. "We have constant touch points with our customers." Chand is responsible for the company's global technology strategy and technical innovation, and leads the company's global R&D operations.

To hear a technologist like Chand talk about "customer touch points" tells you a lot about the culture at Rockwell Automation. Dig deeper into what makes Rockwell tick, and you'll find a customer-success mind-set embedded into every part of the business, from the executive suite to the factory floor. Even Chand's official corporate bio states that the CTO "focuses on making a difference for customers by helping them achieve greater productivity and sustainability."

Customer-Centric Leader

In our view, Rockwell Automation stands out as one of the true leaders of the customer-first revolution. Like all the customer-centric companies we've profiled in *Competing for Customers*, Rockwell has woven customer success into the fabric of its corporate culture. And as you'll see in this chapter, its business has thrived in part because of its commitment to measuring what success means for its customers.

In a sense, Rockwell's customer-first culture arose as the natural by-product of the company's day-to-day business activities. Most of the company's big factory installations take years to build and refine, necessitating close and frequent interactions with customers and careful listening habits. "The automation investment lifecycle of design, operate, and maintain tends to be longer, 10 years plus," Chand told us.

Keeping these systems running over the long haul explains why Rockwell's services arm plays such a prominent role in the business. The organization works with customers to continuously optimize installed automation systems as well as the enterprise itself. Rockwell's services business also serves as a listening post, capturing insights about customers' likes and dislikes, and what they could do to take operations to new levels of efficiency and productivity. "Through our services business, we have direct knowledge of areas where customers could benefit," Chand says. "For example, if they implemented a more secure network, how could they improve safety and productivity in their brownfield plants?"

To augment its intelligence gathering on the manufacturing floor, Rockwell circulates customer surveys and hosts advisory boards where it collects feedback about Rockwell's products and strategic road maps. Periodic safety and regulatory assessments also act as triggers for customers to think about new investments and how to update their investments to get more value from an existing solution. Thus, Rockwell turns what is normally an obligatory routine into an opportunity to gather insights and create value.

Quantifying Value

Although close listening has given the company a good idea of what customers want, how does it know whether it's delivering the goods? That's where the art of measuring business value comes in—something that Rockwell has mastered in recent years as customers have started insisting on seeing positive ROI from every investment. "In the past, we could just go to a customer and say, 'Hey, we can provide you value,' but not support that with any quantification," Chand says. "That's not true anymore. There's a huge focus in our company around measuring and quantifying how our customers benefit. We almost never sell products that land at the customer's door and you walk away."

In most cases, Rockwell dispatches a "solutions team" to the project site to oversee the integration of Rockwell's products and software with the customer's factory floor; then the team sticks around until all the systems are running smoothly. These implementation projects provide a close-up view into the customer's operations and supply Rockwell with realistic data to accurately estimate the likely impact of the investment. Based on these projects, Rockwell has compiled a library of case studies that quantify the value realized by customers in industries ranging from oil and gas and automotive, to consumer packaged goods and food and beverage.

Organized by industry, the solution teams have deep knowledge of the customers' applications and focus solely on helping the customers successfully achieve their automation goals. Rockwell Automation also provides services ranging from telephone support to onsite services. Services are sometimes billed on a quality-of-service performance metric such as the uptime of assets.

Rockwell's Four Measures of Success

Rockwell Automation routinely tracks four critical indicators of customer success:

- **Faster time to market.** Whether it's an automobile or a beverage, manufacturers want to get to market as fast as possible. That means reducing the time it takes to move from design to production. Companies turn to Rockwell's control and information technology to speed every phase of the process.

- **Lower total cost of ownership.** "A lot of customers don't really think through total cost of ownership," Chand says. "Many focus on procurement cost only." The proper way to view production costs is over the lifetime of an investment, which for a Rockwell factory-automation system can stretch over 20 or even 30 years. Rockwell helps customers understand what these costs are and plan for lowering production costs systematically through smart practices like designing an efficient energy footprint.

- **Improved asset utilization.** "This is all about trying to get to the goal of zero downtime," Chand explains, noting the significant costs incurred when a plant goes offline. In an automobile factory, for example, downtime can run into multiple millions of dollars per hour. To maximize utilization, Rockwell runs remote simulations and installs Internet-connected "smart assets" to predict and avert failures before they happen. "We're using the Internet of Things to actually listen to how our products and solutions are being used," he says.

- **Enterprise risk management.** Rockwell's customers face escalating business risks, everything from the threat of cyber attacks to complying with a maze of safety regulations such as maintaining detailed records for pharmaceutical and food production. Rockwell works to quantify these risks and helps customers create a system that provides the least amount of enterprise risk. "That's a key area where we offer very tangible benefits to our customers," Chand says.

Transformational Vision

Thanks to new technology that seamlessly integrates production and business systems, Chand says that manufacturers now find themselves on the cusp of a new era of efficiency that will boost nearly every measure of success, including the four that Rockwell routinely tracks: time to market, total cost of ownership, asset utilization, and business risk.

Lately, the chief technologist finds himself spending more time with customers talking about "the connected enterprise"—a concept founded on the idea of linking factories, suppliers, and headquarters with a single real-time network, and getting rid of operational "islands" that slow reaction time. "The day when companies built standalone factories that run on their own is ending," Chand says. "More and more factories are now connected with business systems, so you have a good pulse on customer demand, on inventories, on your supply chain. When all that information is tied together with what's going on in your factories, you can optimize your production. We call this integrated control and information."

In partnership with networking leader Cisco, Rockwell is now helping customers build flexible factories that maximize revenue by automatically producing more of what's being consumed at any moment in time. And if a piece of equipment shows signs of failing, you simply check your online supply network for spare parts and immediately produce what's running low, thus maximizing uptime. "There are a lot of things you can do to optimize your production based on information in other parts of the enterprise," Chand says. "This is a vision that enables rapid value creation and resonates really well with our customers."

Shifting Landscape: From CAPEX to OPEX

As the customer-first revolution continues to unfold and more businesses adopt cloud subscription services, customers are moving from a capital expenditure (CAPEX) to an operating expense (OPEX) approach to investing. For businesses buying technology and other services, this can offer a significant advantage: You avoid tying up cash in an investment that may not pay off for years, if ever.

At the same time, the shift toward pay-as-you-go OPEX purchasing models puts more pressure on the seller to retain customers from year to year. And to do that, sellers need to ensure that their customers are achieving the business outcomes or business value they are expecting. Constant measurement of value realization is essential in these scenarios—and Rockwell is acutely aware of this.

"That's definitely in line with the trends we are seeing," says CTO Chand. "It's really pay as you go and use as you need." He notes that shifting to the OPEX model is "still in the early stages" among industrial enterprises, but more are experimenting with subscription business models, including software-as-a-service and product-as-a-service. "We see that need emerging in our market as the move to connected smart assets picks up momentum," he says.

Considering that the lifecycle of Rockwell's systems can span more than a decade, it's no coincidence that Rockwell excels at keeping customers onboard, and its marketing and sales practices reflect its commitment to never walking away from customers. "Our marketing is not really aimed at just adding more customers," Chand says. "It's also aimed at building thought leadership with existing customers. Whenever we have a new technology, we also provide our customers either a clear migration plan from what they currently have, or how they could adopt the new technology with what they currently have."

The accelerating trend toward new revenue models is spurring Rockwell to think more creatively when it comes to driving customer loyalty and retention. One idea would be to link the fees it charges customers to the actual business outcomes they experience—a pricing strategy that more and more companies are contemplating these days.

One example Chand envisions might be to promise a customer a 10% reduction in electric costs in exchange for a percentage of those savings. The CTO says that Rockwell is "experimenting with these types of models" even though he doesn't see them becoming widespread in the automation industry—not yet anyway. "But they are definitely emerging," he says. By virtue of its customer-first culture and value-measuring prowess, Rockwell is ideally positioned for when the industry is ready to embrace innovative pricing models linked to business outcomes.

10

Creating a Blueprint for Customer Success

"Our DNA is as a consumer company—for that individual customer who's voting thumbs up or thumbs down. That's who we think about. And we think that our job is to take responsibility for the complete user experience. And if it's not up to par, it's our fault, plain and simply."

—Steve Jobs

Customer success has gone from a slogan in the software-as-a-service industry to a capability we believe all businesses must acquire. We hope that we have made a strong case in this book for customer success delivery while also showing what leaders of customer success look and act like. But let's be clear: mastering the art of customer success delivery can't be purchased off the shelf or left to a few mid-level managers to implement. Rather, customer success is a transformational journey, one that can be taken by every type of organization, from "born in the cloud" startups to long-established "born before the cloud" enterprises to organizations that have absolutely nothing to do with the cloud. We'll give you a feel for what these transformative journeys look like in the next two chapters.

But how do you successfully navigate your own journey? How do you get to the point where every part of your organization is geared to customer success, so that delivering it becomes an orchestrated, disciplined, and almost natural instinct? In other words, (forgive the cliché but it's apt): How do you make customer success part of your company's DNA? That's what this chapter is all about.

Throughout this book we have talked about how the activities in the three pillars of customer success are unique to each phase of your customers' lifecycle. Figure 10.1 illustrates what a leading *customer success delivery* capability might look like as key actions you would take to advance customers toward successful business outcomes.

	Listen	Engage	Ensure
Define (Set Requirements and Select)	• Demonstrate commercial ease of doing business • Understand needs	• Demonstrate the ability to be a trusted advisor • Apply use cases and build business justification	• Identify desired business outcomes, KPIs, and map to solution
Buy (Acquire and Implement)	• Establish listening posts • Establish ongoing strategic dialog	• Establish governance model and joint account planning process • Agree on solution adoption and change management approaches	• Focus acquisition and implementation processes on business outcomes to reinforce measures of success
Use (Run and Maintain)	• Collect consumption/adoption status • Assess project success	• Track adoption, course corrections • Track ROI incrementally against business case	• Implement change management and adoption measures
Succeed (Create Results)	• Assess realization of business outcomes	• Conduct quarterly business reviews to assess progress by project and business outcomes	• Document and celebrate business outcomes

Source: Competing for Customers, 2016

Figure 10.1 Orchestration of customer success through the lifecycle.

To achieve this level of orchestration, your organization needs to create a blueprint that helps guide your business from its current state to a position where every action is taken with one goal in mind: customer success delivery. That requires making customer success part of your corporate DNA.

The Four "Ps" of the Customer Success Blueprint

To make customer success part of your corporate DNA, we believe you will need to drive operational changes across four key aspects of your business: Planning, People, Processes, and Platforms—what we call the "Four Ps" of the Customer Success Blueprint (see Figure 10.2). These are the underlying "genetic" changes you'll need to make to close your capability gaps.

We begin by outlining these key building blocks and then show how you can transform individual operations within your business with an eye to mastering customer success delivery.

Planning

Think of customer success planning as the ability to define and articulate your vision and associated strategic initiatives that will drive successful business outcomes for your customers. Organizations serious about customer success should work diligently to develop a deep understanding of their customers' business challenges and translate that understanding into plans capable of delivering measurable business results. There are a number of mechanisms and processes you can use, such as collaborative account planning and executive sponsorship, which we highlight in Chapter 7, "Ensure." The key to remember, however, is that this is not a one-time thing. In practice, it's a recurring cycle in which you will need to constantly add value and adapt to your customers' evolving business needs year after year.

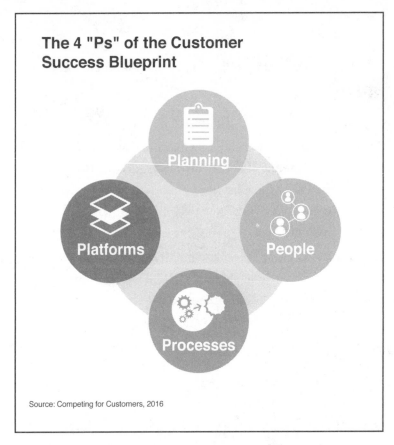

Figure 10.2 The four "Ps" of the Customer Success Blueprint.

As we showed earlier, most companies see themselves as customer-centric and believe that they care about customers. But a real customer success plan is not just about tracking measures of customer satisfaction and loyalty. It is about the entire organization, every department, being focused on the success of its customers. Being customer-centric means that you put your customers first and that you listen to their feedback. Focusing on the customer success plan also means that you are constantly putting yourself in your customers' shoes and asking, how can you make your customers more successful? How can you help them achieve their desired business outcomes?

Everything outlined in the three pillar chapters, Chapter 3, "Listen," Chapter 5, "Engage," and Chapter 7, "Ensure," has a common goal: to help your organization create, manage, and fulfill your customer success plans. If you succeed in executing these plans, you will move your company from being a transactional vendor to an actively engaged, strategic partner with access to your customers' executives and even their boardroom.

To fully achieve customer success, these activities cannot just be the domain of the chief customer officer and customer success delivery teams. Every department has a role to play and therefore a thoughtful "People" strategy is required.

People

To weave customer success into the fabric of your company's culture, everyone in your organization should clearly understand the business outcomes your customers are seeking and be empowered and incentivized to help achieve those outcomes.

In any business it's easy to get hamstrung by political barriers that permit only a few designated individuals or groups to interact with the customer. In a customer success enabled organization, however, every department works together to help customers achieve their business goals. Therefore a new organizational structure is likely called for, one that enables people to do the following:

- Understand each customer's success plan and articulate the journey to achieve it, both internally and to the customer.
- Report on your contributions to customer successes and failures on an ongoing basis.
- Analyze and act on customer data that is most relevant to enhancing customer success.
- Link the value of customer success activities to your agreed-on performance metrics with your internal executives and key customer stakeholders.
- Generate excitement and momentum in every department to ensure close coordination in helping the customer achieve its desired business outcomes.

We explained earlier in the book how each component, or pillar, of customer success delivery requires a distinct set of skills. *Listening*, the foundation for success, requires specialized teams with data analytics expertise. *Engaging* requires executive-level relationship management and strategic consultative skills. *Ensuring* success requires industry acumen and performance measurement skills, to name a few. We have also argued that to thrive in the Subscription Economy, you will need specialized retention management and lifecycle management capabilities to nurture your customers along their journey and accelerate their path to fulfill the customer's business objectives.

With these capabilities, expertise, and motivations in place, the people in your organization will be primed for customer success delivery. The next piece of the puzzle: We believe that new business processes will need to be established to guide the behavior of your teams and help them execute effectively over the long run.

Processes

Establishing coordinated business processes is key to mobilizing the people of your organization behind a common customer success plan. Such *process DNA* allows you to integrate the necessary customer success activities—listening, engaging, and ensuring—across departments with minimal friction. We saw this at the cloud-logistics company Telogis, where the CEO literally built the company around a customer success framework. Of course, many large enterprises don't have the luxury of starting from scratch, but the impact of creating customer success process DNA is equally compelling.

Process DNA helps you pass information quickly between teams and orchestrate a chain of events that keeps everybody focused on customer success. For example, imagine a sales conference in which a group of top customers expresses a preference for your competitor's new product. Without processes in place to pass that feedback along to other parts of your organization—such as product development, marketing, sales, and support—your business as a whole will fail to respond in a coordinated fashion to this breaking news. A critical opportunity will have been missed.

Integrating your *listening processes* with your *engagement processes* spurs you to work more closely with customers to understand why your solution may be falling short. Without those linkages, you may never fully grasp the customer's dissatisfaction or find the right person in your organization to initiate communications and deploy fixes in a timely fashion. Similarly, to convince top customers to stay loyal over the long haul, you will need well-defined *ensuring processes* that links your value-tracking programs with follow-up efforts to communicate the results to the right customer audience. As we outline in Chapter 11, "How Oracle Focuses on Customer Success," these feedback processes take time to develop and must be matched with the right people to ensure that the customer sees the value.

Mapping and documenting new customer success processes will help produce consistent customer experiences. Too often, customer interactions become disjointed, which can lead to sending out mixed messages. Implementing unified, enterprise-wide processes can remove common customer engagement pitfalls, such as sales teams competing for the same customer's attention, dropped handoffs between teams, or bombarding customers with repetitive questions.

To eliminate such confusion and crossed wires, companies need to ensure that all customer-facing representatives follow the same playbook. Coordinating processes and customer data across functional boundaries will ensure that all customer success stakeholders—which should include a broad swath of your organization—work in tandem to achieve the ultimate result: the customer's success.

Platforms

At the beginning of this book, we highlighted some of the big technology developments that are impacting B2B companies today, including the Internet of Things, social media, and big data. Our research found that companies on the forefront of customer success delivery are taking maximum advantage of these innovations to forge new connections with customers. The good news is that there is an abundance of technologies available to the ordinary business that will help them automate and scale their customer success programs. Now more than ever, technologies are available to the smallest and largest organizations alike, thanks to the cloud. These technologies include:

- Customer success management platforms
- Customer experience applications
- Marketing and social media automation tools
- Content management tools
- Internet of Things (IoT) platforms
- Big data analysis tools
- ROI and business case analysis tools

These platforms help customer success-centric companies gather customer insights while also deepening customer relationships and creating new ways to work together. For example, a customer success platform can warn you of a customer whose satisfaction rating—or "health score"—might be worsening, and then automatically send an e-mail to let the customer know you're aware of their issues and are actively working on a solution. Such platforms can be geared to capture, manage, monitor, and act on a whole range of customer success measures, ensuring that you're reaching out for the right reasons, at the right time, and through the right channel. Frequently, we've seen this type of systematic response start a conversation and spark actions that can rescue the relationship. Moreover, customer success platforms are a great way to engage the broader, less profitable, segments of your customer base without breaking the bank.

DNA Mapping for Your Business

Your plan to create a customer success culture will likely start in one corner of the business, such as sales, and move into other operations as the company begins to see the value that a customer success delivery model can bring. In most cases, you can begin wherever you like and expand in any direction that makes sense. It's like a jigsaw puzzle: You can start anywhere and jump around the board, but in the end all the pieces fit together and give you the full picture.

You will also find that parts of your business may evolve or "mature" at different rates, as they test out new operating models centered around customer success and learn new ways of interacting with customers. Let's look at how this evolution typically plays out across key functions of the business, with an emphasis on the four Ps of the customer success blueprint.

Sales

As shown in Figure 10.3, sales organizations often start off as high-priced order takers but soon realize that sustaining growth will require deeper relationships with their customers. As they begin to reorganize around customer success, sales teams learn to sell not just products and features, but complete solutions configured to meet the customer's unique business challenges. The most mature and innovative sales teams may craft deals that actually tie revenue—and commissions—to the customer's achievement of specific business outcomes. These scenarios are unique and require sophisticated pricing and service skills, but when executed correctly they can help build enduring relationships held together by bonds of mutual business incentives.

As sales organizations evolve, they will play a larger role in defining how customers measure success. To develop this understanding, teams should be empowered to establish executive listening posts, develop thought-leadership messaging, and create strategic business cases that demonstrate the business value customers can realize from any given investment.

Figure 10.3 Sales customer success maturity levels.

Sales executives, for their part, must properly encourage and reward teams for implementing customer success-based capabilities. We saw this in the cases of Cisco and GE Power, both of which are rejuvenating their sales teams with an eye to fostering longer-term, subscription-based relationships. But, as we'll describe in our profile of Oracle in the next chapter, this cannot be at the expense of quarter-by-quarter sales quotas but as an additional incentive with longer-term payoffs.

We are now seeing more sales organizations investing in tools to help build and manage customer success activities (see Table 10.1). These can include business case platforms that help generate ROI models, online sales playbooks to deliver consistent value-based messaging, and sales force automation tools to help consolidate and provide visibility into customer touch points.

Table 10.1 Transforming Sales into a Customer Success Organization

The 4 Ps	Actions
Planning	• Set up executive listening posts. • Build thought leadership resources and messaging. • Develop business case capabilities to demonstrate value creation.
People	• Learn to sell not just products and features but coordinated solutions to meet unique customer challenges. • Create direct sales roles or overlays to build more strategic, long-term relationships.
Processes	• Reward sales teams for developing and nurturing customer success-driven relationships. • Consider crafting deals that link revenue to customer business outcomes. • Don't ignore sales quotas—strike a balance between near-term and longer term objectives.
Platforms	Consider investments in: • Business case platforms that help generate and track ROI assessments. • Online sales playbooks to deliver consistent value-based messaging. • Sales force, opportunity management, and account management tools to provide broad visibility and orchestrate customer touch points.

Marketing

As illustrated in Figure 10.4, early-generation marketers have been stuck in a features-and-functions mindset. To evolve, marketing organizations are learning to focus on customer engagement as a means to building more personal relationships and ultimately greater loyalty.

Figure 10.4 Marketing customer success maturity levels.

True customer success marketers take it a step further, concentrating their efforts on customer retention and spotlighting the business outcomes customers can expect to see from day one and over a lifetime (see Table 10.2).

Table 10.2 Transforming Marketing into a Customer Success Organization

The 4 Ps	Actions
Planning	• Focus on strategic planning beyond lead generation and maturation. • Take responsibility for thought leadership, strategic market positioning, and market segmentation. • Share relevant and authentic content via social and mobile channels. • Systematically engage customers long after the first sale. • Introduce programs for promoting long-term retention and loyalty.
People	Acquire skills that allow you to: • Interact more closely with sales, engineering functions, and customers. • Develop and engage in customer forums and communities. • Engage with top customer executives to understand customer pain points, opportunities, and value realized.
Processes	• Use evidence-based marketing to demonstrate ability to deliver quantified ROI results. • Develop detailed customer persona profiles, messaging, and awareness/lead generation workflows. • Establish research analyst-quality content management processes and retention marketing programs. • Integrate these processes with other supporting functions such as sales, services, support, and the executive suite.
Platforms	Consider investments in: • Marketing automation and content management solutions. • Social media automation platforms to establish online communities of interest and brand-building messaging.

Marketing in the era of the Customer First Revolution is no longer focused solely on lead generation—or the "top of the funnel"—although that role will never go away. Now marketers are taking on greater responsibility for thought leadership and strategic market positioning, and they are vigorously responding to what modern B2B customers really want: evidence of your ability to deliver real, measurable business results.

Marketers are also adapting to the stark realities of the Subscription Economy in which deals are never truly final but continuously managed based on vendor performance. Marketers therefore must continue to engage customers long after the first sale and nurture the relationship in creative new ways, including sharing of relevant and authentic content via social-mobile channels. In the new era, marketers are scrambling to hone new skills, including how to promote long-term retention and loyalty, and how to spark conversations that explore strategic transformations.

Because of the nature of retention marketing—requiring, for example, the constant monitoring of customer health measures—business workflows will need be closely integrated with other lines of business that also touch the customer, such as sales, professional services, support, and of course the executive suite. This is also where new marketing platforms come into play: automating marketing campaigns and interactions, content management, and social media programs to help marketers get closer to customers both before and after the contract is signed. A new breed of automated content marketing platforms, for example, allow marketing teams to produce content tailored to individual buying personalities or "personas," and orchestrate tailored customer communications with only a modest staff. Similarly, automated social media platforms help marketers establish online communities and spread brand awareness at a fraction of the cost of conventional marketing programs.

Professional Services

Professional services organizations are the unsung heroes of B2B manufacturers and technology providers worldwide. They are the engineers, consultants, and project managers who do the heavy lifting after the deal is inked. They install the product, fine tune it, and do the necessary troubleshooting and tweaks until the systems—from sophisticated business software to heavy industrial equipment—are humming along. In years past, that's when most professional services teams went home and on to the next job.

With the Subscription Economy and the Customer First Revolution bringing a new focus on delivering business outcomes, that routine is changing and professional services organizations are adapting and maturing accordingly, as shown in Figure 10.5.

Figure 10.5 Services customer success maturity levels.

No longer mere "implementers" of hardware and software, the new professional services organization is becoming a key player in the larger mission of retaining customers and ensuring that every customer is deriving maximum business value from its investment. In short, professional services organizations are becoming less tactical and more strategic (see Table 10.3).

Table 10.3 Transforming Services into a Customer Success Organization

The 4 Ps	Actions
Planning	• Add capabilities to support managed services, operations, and management consulting to build strategic-level business cases and deliver change management services. • Team with the sales organization in leading workshops and executive briefings. • Drive strategic consultative engagements with the top level customer executives • Become the "point of the spear" linking a solution's potential value to the customer's business purpose.
People	• Shift focus from individual products to complex solutions, industry-specificity, and business value. • Learn to manage and monitor service levels, incremental value realized, and the health of customer relationships. • Communicate strategic value propositions; document and package results for executive audiences. • Blueprint and monitor the customer success journey.
Processes	• Migrate process to support ongoing operations vs. "one-and-done" consulting engagements. • Implement scorecards to communicate and track business results. • Enable customer visibility into the success of projects to support renewal decisions. • Add customer success services, such as adoption, performance, and value-realization services to generate new revenue streams.

The 4 Ps	Actions
Platforms	Consider investments in:
	• Value delivery automation solutions to create a structured, standard way to communicate business cases.
	• Build a central library of value results and benchmarks to share with marketing.
	• Link project management tools with other systems that track customer milestones and business outcomes.

The evolving professional services role comes on the heels of the growing trend towards managed services and hosting, where implementers hand over responsibilities to operational teams to run the systems on behalf of the customer. Consequently, more providers, including systems operators, are being "embedded" in customer operations. This places them in a great position to spot opportunities for improving processes and adding value for customers over time. These opportunities can often be best addressed by professional services team members, given the alignment of requisite skills.

We are seeing more companies seize this moment to reinvent their professional services groups—for instance, by teaming them with sales and marketing to help monitor customer health, scout new opportunities, and incubate trusted advisor relationships that can translate into long-term strategic partnerships. As a result, companies are beefing up their professional services organizations with management consultants and customer success managers capable of building business cases for outcomes-focused initiatives. In fact, we are seeing more services professionals picked to lead workshops, run executive briefings, and even spearhead multimillion-dollar strategic engagements.

As professional services team members become more deeply embedded in customer organizations, new processes will be needed to manage their work, which will shift from "one-and-done" installations to engagements that are iterative and ongoing, blending implementers with operators. Such engagements can include scorecards and progress reports to give the customer visibility into business results and link them to subscription-renewal decision points. In this way, professional services organizations can contribute significantly to ensuring renewal revenue streams.

Technology will quickly evolve to better support the enhanced role of professional services teams, which now routinely share automation platforms with sales and marketing groups. Unified platforms will help enforce standard ways of communicating business cases, and as solutions are deployed, will help marketers capture results to create evidence-based marketing assets.

Customer Support

Support organizations and operations are evolving in line with other parts of the business in the customer-first era, with the call center and technical support teams of the future shaping up to be entirely different from what exists today. Customer success DNA is finally being infused into the much-maligned customer support function, and the results are impressive. It turns out call center agents and technical support staff can be among your best brand champions, drivers of renewal revenue, and so much more.

As companies re-orient around customer success, support operations will take on new roles and responsibilities. As shown in Figure 10.6, customer support historically has been about taking calls when products break and mobilizing resources to implement a fix. More mature operations can troubleshoot progressively more complex systems—not just individual products or pieces of equipment, but broader solutions composed of multiple integrated products. These basic services are the bread and butter of call centers and technical support everywhere.

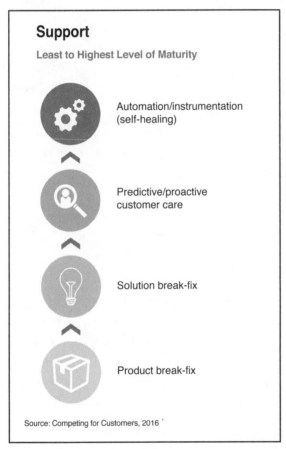

Figure 10.6 Support customer success maturity levels.

In an effort to become even more customer-success focused, we are now seeing customer support go a step further: predicting and solving problems before they happen (see Table 10.4).

Table 10.4 Transforming Customer Support into a Customer Success Organization

The 4 Ps	Actions
Planning	• Look beyond managing internal service level agreements (such as time to resolution) to external commitments that align with the operation of your customer's business. • Develop a deeper understanding of how the customer is using your products.
People	• Acquire skills to manage and support higher-order customer issues that span your products and even include other providers' products. • Develop new support resources that can predict issues and work proactively to course-correct.
Processes	• Drive tighter integration with other functions (sales, marketing, professional services, product development). • Establish procedures to anticipate issues based on mining earlier experiences and root cause analysis.
Platforms	• Consider investments in solutions for an omni-channel customer service experience, tied to the other aspects of the customer lifecycle. • Use customer service platforms as "listening posts" to gauge customer success and identify engagement opportunities. • Consider adding IoT-based predictive care platforms that monitor and react to product usage and performance.

Technology has been a driving force in this transition. Thanks to the Internet of Things, more products are now being equipped with self-monitoring sensors that can predict failures and implement fixes, helping reduce the volume of service requests. Plus, the centers themselves are getting more efficient, featuring self-learning knowledge bases that help agents get to the bottom of problems in a fraction of the time. All of these advancements are allowing support teams to take on higher-level duties, such as proactively communicating with customers when a product might be prone to fail, and offering advice on a range of business-efficiency matters.

The new consulting-type role for support operations dovetails with customer success-centric companies like Rockwell Automation, profiled in the previous chapter, whose support staff are frequently "embedded" in the customer's operations and responsible for keeping mission-critical production systems running non-stop. For these support teams, it's essential to approach problems from a more systemic and strategic perspective, and spot opportunities for improving underlying production and business processes. This is when customer support turns into a true driver of business outcomes and customer success.

It's no surprise we're seeing the skill sets of many support staffs being upgraded to fit a more customer success-focused business model. These organizations are also redesigning business flows and adding digital platforms to better integrate support teams with the broader business, including product development, sales, and professional services (see Table 10.4). We expect these platforms to continue to expand their usefulness by integrating with many of the sales enablement and customer experience solutions available today. Platforms will continue to play a critical role in customer success because support interactions serve as vital listening posts and engagement channels.

Product Development

Steve Jobs is famous for saying that Apple often defines the customer's needs by designing products the customers didn't even know they wanted. Increasingly, B2B companies will find opportunities to do the same as they become more and more customer success savvy. Indeed, companies like Oracle, Telogis, GE, and Rockwell are all doing that with their customers today. Product development organizations must live, breathe, and eat customers' strategic plans to ensure the long-term success of the enterprise.

Fortunately most product designers already have the *technical skills* to take on the demands of customer success delivery. That's the good news. But what many product developers lack are the *people skills* needed to collaborate with a broad set of non-engineers in the design of a new generation of products specifically engineered to deliver business results. These skills include the ability to *carefully listen* to sales teams, marketers, consultants, and support professionals in a joint effort to understand the nuances of an industry or functional domain and then design products to innovate and increase competitiveness. People skills also include the ability to *interact directly with customers* to show commitment to their success and factor their perspectives into the next generation of products.

As depicted in Figure 10.7, product development will evolve in the Customer First Revolution, from an initial focus on product designs to more integrated solution designs, and then ultimately to co-developed solutions designed from the ground up to deliver business outcomes.

We believe the spread of the Internet of Things (IoT) will create new product-design opportunities, allowing for features like remote product monitoring, proactive support, and self-healing. Developers will benefit by gaining technical acumen in cloud-based application development, integration, security, and management. See Table 10.5.

Figure 10.7 Product development customer success maturity levels.

Table 10.5 Transforming Product Development into a Customer Success Organization

The 4 Ps	Actions
Planning	• Engage customers in product road map development sessions.
	• Partner with key customers across key industries in quarterly business reviews and strategic planning sessions.
People	• Gain skills to work with a broad set of non-engineers to design solutions from a holistic customer experience perspective, based on collaboration with sales, marketing, consultants, and support.
	• Learn to exploit data streaming from IoT-enabled products.
	• Develop technical acumen with cloud-based application development, security, orchestration, and operations.

The 4 Ps	Actions
Processes	• Develop processes to engage customers over entire customer lifecycle.
Platforms	Consider adopting: • IoT and big data analytics platforms to find new ways to improve products. • Industry standards for applications integration, system management, and top-level orchestration.

If product developers hope to emulate Steve Jobs and create products that customers don't even know they need—delivering tremendous value nonetheless—they will need to focus relentlessly on industry dynamics and understanding customer business challenges and opportunities. This will require better processes for engaging customers as the relationship evolves over time. Thus the designers of next-generation products should spend a portion of their time "in market," assessing the ever-changing needs of customers, anticipating market shifts, and being an evangelist for the company's future.

Customer success-driven product developers will be eager consumers of IoT and big data analytics platforms that allow them to tap into volumes of product usage and performance data, fueling innovation. The teams will also benefit from the myriad of other platforms described earlier, including sales enablement and evidence-based marketing tools that track and quantify business impacts; customer success platforms that provide real-time access to product performance at customer sites; and customer service platforms that track and manage solution issues.

Change Management

How do you change status quo thinking when it comes to customer success delivery? It's not enough to simply appoint a chief customer officer or vice president of customer success. It has to start at the very top. The CEO needs to set the example by spending time engaging with customers and learning what business needs they're trying to address. The board of directors should also provide an outside-in view of the strategic value the company is delivering to the markets it serves. The whole executive team should be driving customer success and passion throughout the organization, taking personal responsibility for overseeing success at selected customers. Yes, a chief customer officer can be a powerful force to drive this purpose throughout the organization. But as you'll see in our profile of Oracle's journey, there is a lot more than just a single leader that helps you put customer success into your corporate DNA.

11

How Oracle Focuses on Customer Success

"When our customers are successful, Oracle is successful."

—Mark Hurd, Oracle CEO

Oracle: A Snapshot

"A Relational Model of Data for Large Shared Data Banks" is the title of a paper written in 1977 by Edgar F. Codd, an English computer scientist. That paper purportedly was Larry Ellison's inspiration to build a company called Software Development Laboratories (SDL), which ultimately became Oracle. Today, the company generates nearly $40 billion in revenue, has more than 132,000 employees and 400,000 customers, and operates in more than 145 countries. Oracle invests more than $5 billion annually in research and development and has spent about $60 billion on more than 100 acquisitions of other companies over the past decade. The company produces a broad array of software and hardware products that you will find in corporate and public-sector data centers around the world. Most of these products are also available in the form of cloud services, delivered over the Internet to customers from Oracle's own data centers. See Figure 11.1 for additional Oracle facts and figures.

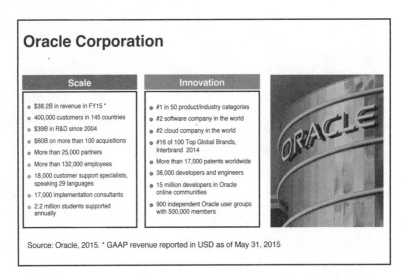

Figure 11.1 Oracle corporation.

The Oracle Customer Success Journey

Oracle has been a technology leader for considerably more than 30 years, and maintaining that position has meant constant, aggressive evolution. The market has not stood still over those decades, and neither have Oracle customers and technology in general. Since Oracle's beginnings, there has been a conflicted, even polarized, view of the company's relationship with customers. Ask a customer about his view of Oracle, and you may well hear "aggressive and a fierce negotiator." You're equally likely to hear "great products, great vision, and our most strategic technology partner." Oracle is all of the above. The company is constantly innovating and pushing the envelope of one of the most competitive industries on the planet. It can also be truly customer-centric. Oracle hasn't always gotten it exactly right, but this story explores Oracle's pursuit of customer success: what has worked, the lessons learned, and where the organization goes from here.

Globalizing Sets the Foundation

Implementing a high degree of centralization and standardization created a platform for much of the actions Oracle has taken in its customer success journey. In the 1990s Oracle was highly decentralized, with businesses run independently at the local level, supported largely by local systems. Seeing the opportunity to gain efficiencies and create a foundation for extraordinary growth, Oracle's then-CEO Larry Ellison mandated that the entire company adopt a single suite of systems (Oracle systems, of course) to run all business processes and to manage related data in a highly centralized fashion. That meant, for example, taking nearly a hundred systems to manage and track Oracle's people down to one single HR system, run worldwide. It also meant that Oracle, from that moment forward, would systematically and completely adopt its own technology to run its business. Oracle became its own biggest and toughest customer, in perpetuity. The product development team became fully responsible for running all the Oracle systems that run the Oracle business. This way, Oracle directly experiences every customer benefit and every pain. The latter can then be fixed, with a lesson learned that benefits all customers.

Building through Complementary Innovation and Acquisition

Oracle's eponymous database was only the start. Since then the company has developed a wide variety of software products spanning the range of technologies that automate businesses. Ellison saw early on that delivering products that are well integrated with each other simplifies the customers' job and yields real value. This proved true with Oracle's suite of business applications, where individual programs were designed to work together, and with the underlying Oracle database.

More than ten years ago Oracle realized that there were opportunities to quicken the pace of innovation and address customers' needs more holistically through carefully targeted acquisitions. The first major acquisition was PeopleSoft, a Pleasanton, California company that specialized in business software for human resources. As Oracle headed into the final weeks and months of its hostile and protracted takeover of PeopleSoft, it's safe to say that the company was looked upon with a lot of skepticism. PeopleSoft customers were worried about how their significant investments would be sustained. Employees and community members were worried about jobs. Investors and business partners worried as well. Even the U.S. government and European Union expressed concerns. The fear was that Oracle would, in the worst-case scenario, simply shut down the PeopleSoft product line to eliminate a tough competitor. Or, less dramatically, Oracle would keep the product line limping along without ongoing innovation, with the value of customers' investments in that technology dwindling over time.

The *Wall Street Journal*, on December 14, 2004, said, "People-Soft Inc. agreed to be acquired for $10.3 billion, capitulating after 18 months of resistance. To seal the deal, Mr. Ellison prevailed over the U.S. government, which sued to block the merger on antitrust grounds. And he defied skeptics who warned that a hostile software takeover couldn't work because the target company's technical and management talent would walk out the door." Oracle's mission became a single-minded focus on PeopleSoft customer retention. Oracle knew that the company had to hold onto every last customer to do the right thing for them, to prove its intentions, and to deliver the reality of Oracle's value proposition to the PeopleSoft business. This value proposition: to invest more and present more value to those customers with the melding of PeopleSoft products and other Oracle core technology and applications.

Since December 2004, Oracle has made more than 100 acquisitions. See Figure 11.2 for a sampling of those purchases. Integrating these businesses into Oracle—and fusing together the products to realize the full potential of those combinations—is a daunting task. Beyond integration of the products, how Oracle sells to and services customers across product lines, geographies, and industries has evolved, and that is key to this story. Acquisitions continue to this day to extend Oracle's offerings by combining technologies that complete process automation, data integration, and decision making capabilities across functional domains and industries.

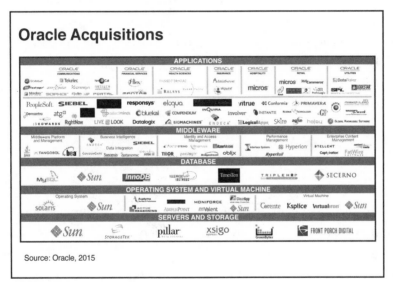

Figure 11.2 Oracle acquisitions.

Specialization Creates Value for Customers

You can't sell everything to everyone. With the diversity of products Oracle has, one sales rep can't possibly be effective in selling Enterprise Resource Planning cloud applications to a customer in the morning and then come back that afternoon and sell middleware, a

Big Data Appliance, or Communications Network Monitoring software. These products and their markets are so different and require such fundamentally different expertise that one person having the full range of conversations with a customer simply isn't viable. Instead, Oracle has implemented a model based on fielding highly specialized customer-facing teams. That specialization means that an account team for one of Oracle's larger, more complex customers can have as many as 20 different product experts. Each team member has a key role to play to support the customer, but having every specialist coming at the customer independently of each other—and of one cohesive strategy—would be chaotic. To mitigate this, Oracle has put in place an account management program for its largest customers, with a key account director and staff orchestrating all the customer-facing Oracle resources. The objective is to present a unified face to the customer, with the Oracle team working in a coordinated fashion guided by the customer's strategic objectives.

Customer Programs for Scale and Consistency

In 2004, the customer loyalty and engagement programs Oracle had in place were rudimentary at best. The company had an elementary customer survey tool and a variety of customer reference programs in place at a regional level. Basic customer feedback was collected, mostly related to product satisfaction. Oracle worked with the happiest customers to create customer references to aid local sales and marketing teams.

As the PeopleSoft acquisition came to fruition, and with a view toward PeopleSoft customer retention, Oracle formed a team that would focus on customer centricity for that part of the business and then for the entire Oracle customer base. The ultimate objective was to develop a coordinated suite of programs focused on delivering an improved customer experience for all customers. Over time, these programs at their core have evolved and have helped Oracle progress down the customer-centricity road and head toward customer success. These are Oracle's key objectives in this journey:

- To assess customer sentiment in every possible way. Oracle completely redesigned its customer feedback efforts by putting in place new survey tools, advanced analytics, and by bringing groups of top customers together on an ongoing basis to solicit and discuss their views of Oracle as a strategic business partner.

- To address the specific issues customers voiced and to do so quickly, transparently, and across all Oracle products and lines of business. This is done under the umbrella of an issue-to-resolution program, applying a common set of tools, processes, and measurements. Included in those resources are implementation success managers and customer success managers, two roles that have been put in place over the past two years. This is where the rubber hits the road in the progression from customer centricity to customer success at Oracle.

- To look at those specific issues and glean from them core themes affecting many customers and then address those themes at the root cause. This is called the Oracle Top Ten Program. Several times a year structured and unstructured customer feedback is gathered and synthesized. The company distills the feedback to ten key themes and then develops a set of suggested root causes, business impact statements, and proposed action plans. Each of those ten themes is assigned, with all the supporting data and suggested paths forward, to the team best equipped to address the issues efficiently and thoroughly. The central customer programs organization works with those teams to refine and execute corrective action plans and ultimately measure the improvement that customers see as initiatives take effect. Figure 11.3 details the Top Ten methodology.

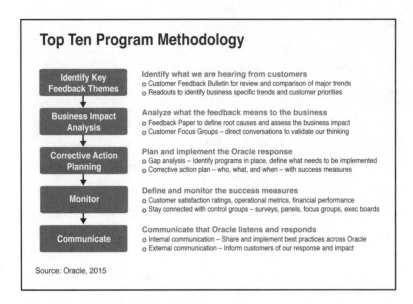

Figure 11.3 Top ten program methodology.

- To communicate across the Oracle customer base about what the company is hearing and what it's doing about it. In the past two years, especially, Oracle has made improvements to its overall customer communications approach. This takes the form of written communications to various customer segments and empowerment of account teams with details that they can communicate to their customers as part of their day-to-day dialog.

- To fix ongoing challenges with account management and ease of doing business. Key accounts and regional lead accounts programs continue to refine Oracle's account management approach for the biggest customers. The ultimate goal of these programs is to help the customer achieve its desired business outcomes and, at the same time, achieve Oracle's business objectives for that account. Done right, this means execution of a true partnership with a high degree of transparency in what both parties need, in the short run and the long run, to get from the relationship. Has Oracle achieved this across all of its biggest customers? No, but significant progress has been made—and over time, more and more customers see the effect of the model in place, as evidenced by some of the "ease of doing business" metrics shown in Figure 11.4. Getting "ease of doing business" right is arguably the most important thing to do to survive and thrive in the Subscription Economy.

Figure 11.4 Ease of doing business.

- To manage a global customer references program, developing Oracle advocates and executing co-marketing efforts on a large scale, capitalizing on everything Oracle does to listen and respond to customers, and recognizing that when we do everything right, those customers view Oracle products and services as an integral part of their success.

Engaged Employees Mean Engaged Customers

In 2012, Oracle CEO Mark Hurd began an intense push on employee satisfaction. When the company compared employee satisfaction data with the customer satisfaction, loyalty, and engagement input collected on an ongoing basis, the team quickly saw that employee pain points matched many of the customer pain points that Oracle had been addressing. This was especially so with "ease of doing business" challenges such as account management, quoting, ordering, delivery, and product support. The initiatives since launched to improve employee efficiency and effectiveness align with many of the core customer-engagement and customer success-related efforts. The principles of employee engagement that influence customer success are depicted in Figure 11.5.

Figure 11.5 Employee engagement.

Key Takeaways: The Oracle Customer Success Journey

1. Use the products and services you deliver—be your own best customer and build what you learn back into those products and services.

2. Communicate early and often that you will protect customer investments forever—and especially for acquired products.

3. Evolve and expand offerings in the context of a single, differentiated, and easy-to-articulate strategy. Be clear about how the strategy creates value for your customers—and communicate that constantly.

4. Orchestrate your account-level strategy and tactics to align with the customer's business objectives, using the customer's language and metrics.

5. Apply one common issue-resolution process and address underlying themes at the root.

6. Place particular focus on the ease of doing business. This has never been more important than in today's Subscription Economy.

7. Put equal emphasis on your business objectives and your customers' attainment of their business objectives. Broadcast across your organization how you are achieving your customers' objectives.

8. Align employee engagement and customer engagement efforts by showing your employees how their actions affect customers—positively and negatively.

Some Serious Challenges

Oracle has made strong progress over the past decade developing and implementing a unique customer-centricity strategy, and more recently, a customer-success strategy. All this while the company has quadrupled in size. A number of factors can work against Oracle, though, and being acutely aware of them will help the company navigate the next steps in its journey. We suspect many other organizations share some combination of these opposing forces.

First, Oracle is a large, complex organization, always growing and evolving. It's a moving target, with new products constantly launched and new companies constantly being acquired and integrated. The whole point of constant evolution is to keep pace with—and ideally stay ahead of—customer needs.

The good news is that Oracle has a steady flow of new products and new capabilities to present to its customers. The bad news is that the dizzying pace is hard for Oracle employees to keep up with. That means it's even harder for Oracle's customers. Add to this the fact that different Oracle teams engage with different buyers and users within the same customer organization, and it gets complicated. In the old days, Oracle generally had one buyer per organization. The CIO had a clear monopoly on the acquisition of technology. Today, Oracle deals with many other buyers—including the CMO, CHRO, CFO, chief architect, and chief security officer—all with different and often competing objectives.

Further, in today's environment the customer truly is king. Taking a page out of new consumer buying patterns, B2B buyers now capitalize on a vast amount of information at their fingertips. The Subscription Economy has radically changed customer expectations in terms of ease of doing business, low-cost solutions, extraordinary amounts of product and provider information available, and the modest cost of switching from one seller to another. The buyer has all the power. Figure 11.6 shows how B2C behaviors and expectations bleed into the B2B customer experience.

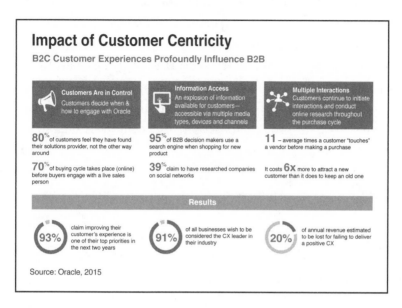

Figure 11.6 Impact of customer centricity.

Lastly, experienced technology buyers are leery of putting all their eggs in one basket. Even if Oracle really does have the single most complete and robust end-to-end solution to deliver, customer perceptions of being locked in can and often do drive decisions to mitigate that perceived risk.

Where Oracle Is Today

As we do throughout this book, Oracle thinks about and pursues customer success in terms of listening, engaging, and ensuring. As the company continues its journey, progress is assessed in each of these areas.

Listening

Oracle has many different listening posts embedded throughout the lifecycle of its customers' experience, all in place to collect and analyze both structured and unstructured input (see Figure 11.7 for the typical Oracle customer lifecycle). Listening spans every aspect of the lifecycle, using different tools with different objectives and different measures. That feedback is reported through Oracle business intelligence tools to provide role-based views into this data across every corner of the company. Summarized results are then distributed to executives quarterly, with a series of more than 100 discussions set up to review results and success measures. Oracle collects a combination of satisfaction, loyalty, and customer success measures, in significant detail, using surveys, customer advisory panels, focus groups, advisory boards, 1:1 customer and account team input, social media postings and chatter, and market research.

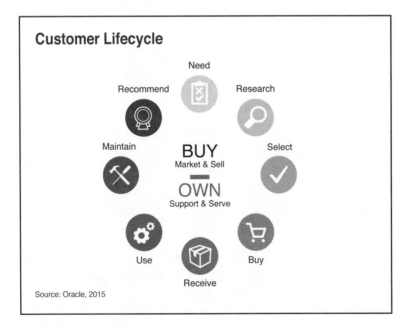

Figure 11.7 Customer lifecycle.

Engaging

Customer engagement is focused on extending relationships and collaboration with customers at both strategic and tactical levels. Putting in place a simple, universal model with a core set of engagement programs and then tracking how customers in fact engage across those programs creates a strong leading indicator of satisfaction, loyalty, and even attainment of business outcomes for those customers. Ideally, engagement occurs at multiple points along the customer lifecycle, with opportunities targeted to specific customers and customer segments based on Oracle's overarching account segmentation strategy. These are the core engagement programs:

- **Customer lifecycle management.** Oracle is implementing a standardized process that guides all cloud customers through a consistent set of milestones from the moment a subscription deal is signed through getting the solution into sustained production and realization of value. This new process is comprised of a standard set of tools, measures, and—most important— standard roles and responsibilities aimed at customer success.

- **Executive advisory boards.** Customers meet regularly with other customers and Oracle senior management to provide input on various aspects of Oracle's strategy, including products, services, and how strategic partnerships are formed and nurtured.

- **Key or regional lead accounts.** These involve structured account management programs that provide a coordinator for all Oracle resources, a core account team, delivery of a collaborative account plan, quarterly business reviews, and harnessing of expertise to map customer business issues, opportunities, and desired business outcomes to Oracle solutions.

- **Technology briefing sessions.** In these sessions customers share their strategies and are updated on a semiannual or annual basis on the current state of Oracle technologies, providing the platform for alignment of customer and Oracle investments and strategies.

- **Executive engagement.** Oracle has a structured approach for planning and executing the interaction between its top executives and customers. Organizations are strategically targeted for different types of executive engagement, based on various criteria, including total addressable spend, alignment of customer direction with Oracle core go-to-market strategies, customer brand value, and desired strategic partnership outcomes.

- **Oracle business case and architectural engagements.** These are three- to five-week consultative engagements in which a technology architecture and business case are developed so that the customer has a detailed road map to follow for adoption of new technologies and achievement of business outcomes.

- **Referencing and co-marketing.** A global customer references and co-marketing program manages how Oracle engages customers as advocates by telling stories about how Oracle contributes to their success.

Oracle analysis has shown that getting customers progressively more engaged in specific programs has a direct effect on generating incremental revenue. Customers that are modestly engaged in specific programs invest as much as three times more in Oracle technology when compared with a purely transactional buyer. If you move further up the engagement scale and look at a highly engaged customer, as in one who is actively advocating for Oracle, that customer will spend nearly ten times more than the purely transactional buyer (see Figure 11.8).

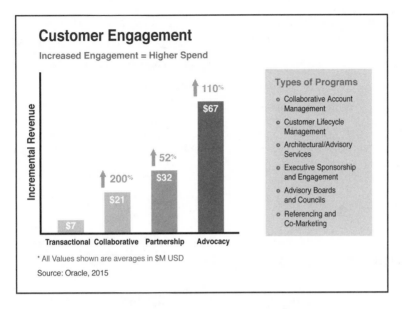

Figure 11.8 Customer engagement.

Ensuring

For certain Oracle customers, the company helps document business value realized and identify opportunities to more fully and successfully adopt the solution delivered. This is a natural extension of the customer lifecycle management engagement activity described earlier.

For Oracle's key accounts, the company holds quarterly business reviews with the customer to track and assess product adoption, customer implementation milestones, and realization of value. Oracle has come to recognize that in order for its customers to be successful in deploying Oracle technology, the company has to work with those customers to incrementally ensure adoption of the solution and establish that value is being realized. This, in turn, drives retention.

In this new economy, retention is king. The math is straightforward: If Oracle were to sell a software license for $1 million and the customer was retained for a decade, the payoff would be about $3 million over those ten years—because of the additional $2 million in support revenue generated in that time frame. If the same customer bought the same product for $500 thousand as a subscription, the ensuing ten years would generate $5 million. The risk of losing a customer subscription over ten years is arguably greater, but the reward is substantial.

What Oracle Has Learned

When Oracle began this journey, the company had no idea where it would lead. The objective at that time was all about customer retention. Along the way, the company realized that customer centricity is a great outcome, but not enough. Oracle has been shifting its focus to customer success over the past 18 months. The progress has been good, but there's still a long way to go.

Some of what Oracle has learned is shown in Table 11.1.

Table 11.1 Some Oracle Lessons Learned

	Lessons Learned
Listening	Listening opportunities are also great for relationship building, especially important for functional "personas" such as CMOs, CFOs, and CHROs.
	An arsenal of customer sentiment data—combining direct input, market research, structured and unstructured data, and third-party influencer views—validates the strategy and helps keep messaging on track.
	Customer engagement, satisfaction, loyalty, and success drivers vary widely across different customer segments.

	Lessons Learned
Engaging	The Oracle customer segmentation strategy has yielded huge benefits in aligning the company and its investment in customers of different shapes and sizes.
	Clear, constant, and timely communication to customers, even without all the answers, is key to building trust and partnership, especially for newly acquired customers.
	Aligning employee feedback with customer input drives improvement in the experience for both, especially for customers.
	Structured executive engagement with customers can make a real difference—and has to be managed carefully to optimize the investment.
	Perfect products and project engagement can be completely undone by "ease of doing business" problems.
	Building a community within Oracle to learn from customer successes and failures moves the needle on customer success faster than anything else.
Ensuring	Ongoing measurement of product adoption, customer project completion, and business outcomes cements a trusted advisor-based partnership—and improves the chances that customers will realize the value they sought.
	Oracle's customers are much better at telling the story of Oracle customer success than Oracle is.
	Connecting the dots between listening, engaging, and ensuring by constantly assessing causes and effects creates a closed-loop system.

What Comes Next

Oracle is especially focused at this juncture on bringing together its internal community of customer success managers, implementation success managers, customer renewal support managers, customer program managers, and customer care specialists. This complex web of experts has overall responsibility for putting into place all the processes, tools, and measures to ensure customer success for the company's fast-growing cloud business. With software-as-a-service and platform-as-a-service bookings growth year-over-year at 200% and an overall cloud revenue run rate at well over $2 billion a year, this is something the company has to get exactly right.

12

The Journey to Customer Success

"Success is a journey, not a destination. The doing is often more important than the outcome."

—Arthur Ashe

As we hope we've made clear in this book, successfully competing for customers in the next decade will require you to master a new set of skills focused on delivering business outcomes that help your customers succeed. We have argued that if you fail to deliver success for your customers, you can expect to suffer from the significant upheavals of an economy that will increasingly thrive on disruption.

We explored the three fundamental capabilities that are essential to producing business success for your customers. These include *listening* closely to your customers, *engaging* them strategically, and finally, *ensuring* specific business outcomes. We also suggested that to excel in each of these areas, you will need to rigorously measure results and continuously adjust your course.

We now conclude the book with some observations about how the ordinary company tackles the job of incorporating customer success into its corporate DNA. No company will get there overnight. It can take years to build these capabilities and put them to work in a fashion that yields measurable results. We call this the *journey to customer success,* and in this final chapter we'd like to help you chart your own unique course and point out some of the key milestones you'll likely encounter along the way.

We characterize the journey as one in which your organization becomes progressively more mature—that is to say, increasingly more focused on and capable of delivering customer success. We'll start by taking a snapshot of where most companies stand today when it comes to mastering the three essential capabilities. After that we'll describe the four stages many companies go through in their journey to customer success—from *satisfier* to *loyalist,* to *collaborator,* and ultimately to *partner.* Finally, we'll provide you with a practical guide in the form of a questionnaire to help your organization design a customer success journey that's right for you.

Listening: From Customer Loyalty to Customer Success

We've found very few companies that haven't made at least a first attempt at setting up listening posts and collecting input from customers. These programs yield useful insights, although most of those insights are in the form of trailing indicators, often months or quarters behind. Virtually all businesses would benefit by implementing a wider array of listening methods and technologies, including those that capitalize on the Internet of Things and analytic tools (including big data) to combine structured and unstructured data into actionable feedback.

The best customer success programs we studied are constantly striving to understand the value they're creating for customers. Figure 12.1 shows the progression in listening sophistication among the companies we looked at.

Figure 12.1 Listening roadmap.

Engaging: From Transactions to Outcomes

We're seeing more organizations shaking up their sales, engineering, services, and even back-office functions to engage with customers more collaboratively and profitably in the fast-growing Subscription

Economy. They are injecting fresh talent into their organizations, and adding new roles to existing account teams to forge the kind of long-term strategic partnerships necessary for driving revenue retention and expansion. Increasingly, organizations are focusing less on acquiring new customers and more on retention, renewals, loyalty, and success.

The face of buyers is changing too, as heads of business units and other C-level executives step up as buyers of technology. Chief operating officers, CMOs, CHROs, and CFOs are acquiring their own IT solutions, no longer relying on the CIO to make these decisions. Coming to grips with the changing *personas* of business buyers remains a challenge for most B2B providers. Also challenging is the new purchaser's penchant for independent research and input from other buyers, sidestepping sales organizations until late in the game.

The best engagers are looking for ways to embed their products and services—and even their people—into customer operations, raising the relationship from mere vendor status to an essential role in the customer's business as a trusted advisor. We believe you've become a trusted advisor when you truly engage your customers and set the stage for a long-term partnership, joint objectives attainment (business outcomes), growth, and profitability. Figure 12.2 shows the typical evolution of a maturing engagement program.

Figure 12.2 Engaging roadmap.

Ensuring: Delivering Value Predictably

We've found very few companies that are making real advancements in *ensuring* customer success. It's an inherently tough thing to do, but something that we believe providers will need to embrace in the years ahead. Software-as-a-service (SaaS) companies are in some cases taking the lead here, in part because the easy-to-switch economics of their business means that customers need to see a predictable, rapid return on their investment.

The Subscription Economy demands a distinct focus on customer retention and success. The need to provide immediate, measurable, and ongoing impact or be shelved is the trial that these companies face every day. As a consequence, some SaaS providers are at least beginning to provide solution adoption and benefits measurement services and are constantly improving the ease of doing business with them.

The leaders in this area are also working to *target* the performance metrics tied to the business outcomes that matter to their customers. Then they will *track* whether customers are hitting those targets and, ultimately, *measure* the resulting positive impact to the business. Perpetually proving value delivered is the holy grail for these companies. Still, for the majority of organizations, ensuring specific business outcomes—and bottom-line results—remains a mostly unexplored frontier in the delivery of B2B products and services. We believe that acquiring this capability will be a key driver of future competitiveness, separating the winners from the losers over the next decade. Figure 12.3 shows key markers on the road to *ensuring* customer success.

Figure 12.3 Ensuring roadmap.

On the Road to Customer Success

Having defined what it means to excel in each of the core customer success capabilities—listening, engaging, ensuring—we can now identify four distinct stages in the journey to customer success. If you are at stage 1, we call you a *satisfier*. The stages that follow depict the *loyalist,* the *collaborator,* and the *partner.* Think of each stage as a maturity level, reflecting your progressive acquisition of customer success knowledge, best practices, and capabilities.

Getting Started: Satisfiers and Loyalists

Most companies today can be classified as either satisfiers or loyalists when it comes to customer success programs. If you see yourself in this category, you have a lot of company.

Listening

Many customer success satisfiers and loyalists show good progress in setting up listening posts, but these efforts are often uncoordinated and don't properly aggregate or analyze the data flowing in. Early-stage listening programs are generally focused on structured feedback (ignoring valuable unstructured information), are reactive in nature, and are designed to bring existing problems to the surface.

These programs invariably lack follow-through mechanisms to facilitate analytics and thorough problem resolution. Satisfiers can usually benefit by consolidating their listening programs, centralizing the data, and developing the analytics that will uncover high-value insights buried in the data. In many cases, satisfiers need to fundamentally alter what they are listening for, focus on customer success versus customer loyalty metrics, and identify early warnings versus after-the-fact distress signals.

How to Get Better

- Focus the questions you ask your customers on how you can enable (or don't enable or even obstruct) your customers' attainment of business objectives and how easy it is to do business with you.

- Take inventory of your listening programs and map them to the strategic goals of your customer success program. Identify gaps, such as mechanisms for picking up on the business benefits your customers are realizing.

- To fill these gaps, devise a plan to add to your existing programs. Be sure to include both structured and unstructured feedback.

- Look at advanced analytics methods and tools for more sophisticated data analysis and reporting.

Engaging

Satisfiers and loyalists have only just begun to understand the value of rethinking engagement for customer success. Some are piloting sales "overlay" teams to alter the nature of engagement and deepen relationships with top customers, but most have yet to push for a similar transformation in marketing, services, support operations, and product development.

It's also common for these organizations to skip critical listening and ensuring design elements, leaving customer success engagements as a disconnected endeavor. Important steps such as defining measurements; tracking solution adoption and key customer-defined milestones; and assessing operational and financial results are too often overlooked.

How to Get Better

- Redesign your customer segmentation strategy and assign the right engagement activities for each group. Don't just look at revenue; apply a more sophisticated model that takes into account total addressable market, share of wallet, customer needs, industry anchor customers, brand value, and strategic impact.

- Deconstruct and reconstruct your account management approach, account team roles and responsibilities, and core customer engagement model.

- Pilot your new engagement model and programs with a small set of key customers, and use the results to introduce refinements.

- Then scale and tailor your program to meet the strategic needs of a broader array of customers, going deeper into your customer base.

- Remember that not all customers need high-touch relationships. Nor can you afford the same level of investment across all customer segments.

Ensuring

Because most satisfiers and loyalists are preoccupied with measuring after-the-fact results, they are generally less attuned at this stage to what it takes to *ensure* business outcomes. That's not to say they don't care about outcomes—they certainly do. But these organizations tend to be so consumed with firefighting that they simply aren't equipped to get sufficiently ahead of the problems to increase the likelihood of customer success.

How to Get Better

- Simply be patient. At this stage, any large-scale initiatives for *ensuring* customer success can usually wait until you more fully develop your listening and engagement programs.

- Telling top customers about your plans to address the challenges and opportunities arising from listening and engaging is a strong first step.

Gaining Traction: Collaborators and Partners

From our experience, the bulk of B2B enterprises acknowledge the critical importance of customer success, and in fact have implemented many of the satisfiers' and loyalists' early lessons. They are indeed beginning to scale and refine their efforts across the enterprise. We classify these companies as customer success collaborators and, ultimately, partners. They are well along the way in establishing the critical tools and capabilities necessary for winning the competition for customers. It's a work in progress, though, to perfect the integration of listening, engaging, and ensuring programs consistently across all customers, all the time.

Listening

Customer success collaborators and partners are steps ahead of the satisfiers and loyalists because they've designed listening programs that start with the end in mind. These programs provide insightful views of their customers' experience that fuel specific actions to ensure outcomes. They also have learned to centralize and coordinate their listening efforts, allowing consistency and easy expansion of programs.

Collaborators and partners are establishing real-time, proactive listening posts so that they can anticipate customer challenges and step in quickly with ideas and solutions. And since they gather data from a huge array of sources—and employ analytical tools to extract key insights—these organizations are becoming valuable repositories of knowledge that customers depend on to find new opportunities to lead in their industries. Because of this, collaborators and partners naturally develop into the role of trusted advisor, gaining a crucial edge in the battle for customers in the Subscription Economy.

How to Get Better

- Turn your listening posts into an early warning system that alerts you to issues that are likely to emerge. This means asking the right questions at the right moments in the customer lifecycle.

- Add advanced analytical capabilities to capture insights hidden in the data, including a clear view of the key drivers of, and impediments to, product adoption and realization of value.

- Systematically use these insights to adjust your segmentation strategy and improve your customer engagement and ensure programs.

- Find creative ways to share operational and key business outcome measures with your customers and apply those to prospects as well.

Engaging

Customer success collaborators and partners organize their customers into segments and create interactions that make sense for each group. These interactions include content marketing, collaborative account management, product adoption, business case and benchmark assessments, executive engagement, and benefits realization programs, to name a few.

Finding the right resources to manage high-level customer relationships is tough, and putting a method in place to consistently forge close top-level executive customer ties can take quarters or years to come to fruition. Collaborators and loyalists begin to engage customers in a coordinated fashion, speaking in a "single voice" to customers across every "touch point"—whether its sales, marketing, support service, or product development driven—clarifying and strengthening the relationship in the process. Similarly, developing compelling thought-leadership marketing content doesn't happen overnight. The most powerful content to be consumed by prospects is that which presents the listen–engage–ensure results from your customers.

How to Get Better

- Develop an account management program that adapts to address different customer segments.

- Put executive engagement programs in place to systematically build top-level relationships that span both line-of-business leaders (such as the head of HR, Sales, or Marketing) and technology leaders (such as the CIO or CTO).

- Define customer success milestones and metrics by customer segment as benchmarks to then be tailored for specific customer situations.

- Extend your engagement model to include joint product development and collaborative planning efforts.

Ensuring

With the right listening posts and engagement processes in place, ensuring success for your customers is now within reach. Collaborators and partners have generally developed effective programs to identify at-risk customers and minimize churn. They've told top customers they're interested in their long-term success but don't necessarily have a comprehensive plan to prove it. Ensuring business outcomes is always a daunting proposition, but these organizations have to build the infrastructure and marshal the resources needed to consistently increase the likelihood of measurable customer success.

Customer success tools and resources typically include technology-enabled programs that monitor and quantify the customer's business results in real time, as well as scorecards that show customers how

well they're performing. The most advanced collaborators and partners are pioneering new revenue models that depend on delivering
business outcomes. Customers, for their part, regard collaborators
and partners as integral to their future success and will share that fact
with prospective customers and investors.

How to Get Better

- Create customer performance scorecards that spell out the
  return on investment for your customers.
- Leverage business case data from sales engagements to calculate the actual return on investment achieved, and then share
  those numbers with the customer along with recommendations
  for achieving more.
- Create tools and content to facilitate development of business
  cases and benefits realization measurement.
- Draw road maps for customers to show them how to fully capitalize on your products and services to meet their strategic goals
  over the next two to three years.
- Push your marketing team to develop and execute campaigns
  based on benefits realized, tailored by industry.

The most successful organizations we examined generally have
advanced listening capabilities, maturing engagement programs, and
relatively nascent ensuring efforts. Figure 12.4 characterizes that as
a collaborator. In this context, we have yet to see a true partner who
has mastered the three pillars of customer success. Our goal in writing this book is to articulate the importance of customer success as we
define it, help you understand where you are in the customer success
journey, and then provide you with targets for where you can and
should be in fully developing your customer success strategy.

Figure 12.4 Four stages of customer success.

The Customer Success Index

How far along is your company in its own customer success journey? To help you find out, we've created the Customer Success Index. Based on a set of questions organized by the three customer success pillars covered in this book, the index can help you assess your organization's current customer success maturity level and formulate a strategy for progressing to the next stage in your journey.

Determining Your Customer Success Maturity Level

Answer the following questions as they pertain to your company by assigning a number of 1 to 5, as detailed here, for each of your responses:

1 = None/No

2 = Minimal/Occasionally

3 = Developing/Frequently

4 = Good/Most of the Time

5 = Great/Always

After assigning a value to each answer, total the value under each pillar (Listen, Engage, Ensure) and then add up the scores across the three pillars for a total score. Using the following scale, you can estimate your current maturity level and identify critical gaps on which to take action:

Satisfier: 0–30

Loyalist: 31–60

Collaborator: 61–110

Partner: 111–150

Customer Success Index Questions

Listening

1. Do you meet with your top customers on a regular basis to get qualitative input on various aspects of your business strategy?

2. Does your understanding of customer needs inform your marketing and sales plays?

3. Have you established listening posts across your customers' lifecycles?

4. Are you measuring customer perceptions of ease of doing business and your ability to effectively provide strategic advice?

5. Does your analysis and reporting of customer feedback provoke action by presenting findings in a compelling way?

6. Do your team members understand what your customers are striving for in business outcomes?

7. Do you understand what business problems or opportunities your customers are solving or pursuing in implementing your solution?

8. Are you assessing customer perceptions of technical and functional project success on an ongoing basis?

9. Are you collecting customer input on solution adoption (number of loyal users)/consumption (number of solution features implemented)?

10. Are you assessing the incremental realization of business outcomes?

Engaging

1. Do you have an enterprise-wide process to communicate your company/solution stories consistently and appropriately at each and every stage of the customer lifecycle?

2. Are you able to tell a story to the customer CxO that would compel this officer to purchase/repurchase your solution?

3. Can you quantify the potential impact of your solution so that budget decisions can be made on a financial/economic basis?

4. Are you having periodic collaborative-solution roadmap sessions to drive new product decisions for your company?

5. Are you viewed as a thought leader in your industry?

6. Have you developed a sales and marketing strategy that focuses on retaining your customers?

7. Does product development have the ability to monitor and react to real-time customer deployment metrics?

8. Do you have the ability to predict and proactively address customer support problems?

9. Is your professional services organization considered a strategic trusted advisor (versus implementation expert)?

10. Do you have the proper systems and tools in place to empower sales, marketing, service, R&D, and support organizations with the big data insights available in the age of IoT/Subscription Economy?

Ensuring

1. Do you regularly help customers improve their solution adoption (number of loyal users) rates?

2. Do you regularly help customers maximize the consumption (number of solution features implemented) of their solution?

3. Do you regularly quantify and communicate the value (e.g., ROI) you have delivered to your top 100 customers?

4. Do you provide services, tools, and programs to regularly help customers achieve the full potential value of their solution?

5. Do you capture and provide best practices and performance benchmarks of your solutions to all of your customers?

6. Do you regularly review and help customers achieve agreed-on milestones and key performance indicators?

7. Do you produce a solution-and-partnership performance dashboard that is reviewed quarterly with customer leadership?

8. Do you have a continuous adoption and value realization program (rather than being a reaction to customer requests)?

9. Do you have a mechanism (including training) to help your channel partners adopt ensuring programs?

10. Do you have a mechanism to feed the results of your ensuring program back to key functional areas (e.g., marketing for reference assets, sales for performance benchmarks/ROI tools, product development for new product prioritization)?

Online Assessment Tool

In conjunction with this book, we're creating an online assessment tool that will automatically calculate your maturity level and highlight critical actions your team can take to advance your own customer success journey. For more information, go to www.competingforcustomers.com.

Index